Feminists and State Welfare

15.95

Carswell /
Methuen

D0147440

Radical Social Policy

GENERAL EDITOR

Vic George

*Professor of Social Policy and
Administration and Social Work
University of Kent*

Feminists and State Welfare

Jennifer Dale and Peggy Foster

Routledge & Kegan Paul
London, Boston and Henley

First published in 1986
by Routledge & Kegan Paul plc

14 Leicester Square, London WC2H 7PH, England

9 Park Street, Boston, Mass. 02108, USA and

Broadway House, Newtown Road,
Henley on Thames, Oxon RG9 1EN, England

Set in Times, 10 on 11 pt
Printed and bound in Great Britain by
Butler and Tanner Ltd, Frome and London

© Jennifer Dale and Peggy Foster 1986

No part of this book may be reproduced in
any form without permission from the publisher,
except for the quotation of brief passages
in criticism

Library of Congress Cataloging in Publication Data

Dale, Jennifer.

Feminists and state welfare.
(Radical social policy)
Bibliography: p.
Includes index.
1. Feminism—Great Britain.   2. Welfare state.
3. Sex discrimination against women—Great Britain.
4. Public welfare—Great Britain—History.   5. Women
and socialism.   I. Foster, Peggy.   II. Title.
III. Series.
HQ1236.5.G7D35   1986   305.4'2'0942   85—11927

British Library CIP data also available

ISBN 0-7102-0278-4 (pb)

Contents

Contents

Acknowledgments

The idea of writing this book grew out of our experience of teaching a course on 'Women and the Welfare State', but without the encouragement of Vic George it might well have remained just another idea. The task of gathering material was greatly eased by our access to the resources – including its most helpful staff – of the EOC Information Centre, one of the few headquarters of a national organization to be located North of Watford. The staff of the Fawcett Library in London were also most helpful in tracking down historical sources. We are grateful to Annie Hudson, Jan Owens and Carolyn Taylor for allowing us access to their unpublished research. The final version of the manuscript has been significantly improved by comments from a number of colleagues and friends. We are particularly grateful to Mikki David, Paul Wilding and Philippa Brewster of RKP for reading the whole draft. Ian Gough, Fiona Williams and Linda Harvey all raised issues which led us to rethink certain aspects of our original analysis. For typing, so patiently and efficiently, the many versions of the manuscript, we thank Jackie Boardman, Enid Roberts and Linda Harvey. Finally we thank our students whose interest in a feminist perspective on welfare provided us with an incentive to keep writing through all the ups and downs of an academic year.

Introduction

'Women and Welfare': these words conjure up a wide range of images. We see women as paid workers within the Welfare State – hospital cleaners, nurses, home helps, social workers – and as unpaid carers within the home, without whom the statutory social services could not function. We also see women as the main users of welfare services both as direct consumers and as negotiators on behalf of other members of their families.

Now let us consider the phrase 'men and welfare'. Our pictures are very different. We see men in well-paid professional and managerial roles. We see them dominating policy making as politicians and top civil servants. We also see men as the leaders of those interest groups – from the BMA to the TUC – to whom social policy makers pay at least some attention.

These contrasting images may be stereotypes but they nevertheless raise a number of key questions about the relationship between women and the Welfare State. Why have women played such a comparatively small role in social policy making? Why is it women, rather than men, who spend so much of their time attempting to negotiate a way through the maze of welfare services? Why are low paid welfare workers predominantly women and high paid welfare professionals and managers mainly men? Who benefits from women's central role as unpaid carers within the family? Who loses out and why?

This book will attempt to answer these questions drawing on feminist theory, research and analysis. It will thus be a book about women and welfare, and a book about feminists' major contribution to our understanding of the Welfare State.

There are, of course, other critiques of the Welfare State which, like feminism, unite theoretical analysis with a commitment to change society. Mainstream social policy analysis was dominated until the 1970s by Fabian approaches which concentrated on inequality in the distribution of the costs and benefits of welfare services. More recently, Marxists have developed a more sophisticated analysis of the way capitalism has constrained and distorted the nature of the Welfare State, and have argued that fundamental changes in the economic system are necessary if the Welfare State is to live up to its promise to meet human need. Finally, some Marxists have moved away from the orthodox emphasis on the quantitative limits to the Welfare State and have reclaimed an older socialist tradition which sees human freedom as dependent upon new forms of social relationships. Their work parallels that of libertarian critics of industrial society who also stress the disabling role of professionals and the sense of powerlessness which modern society induces.

Feminist analysis embraces these concerns and relates them specifically to the position of women. Feminists have looked at sexual inequalities in the distribution of society's material resources. They have explored the complex relationship between capitalism, statutory welfare services, and women's unequal position in the family and at work. They have documented the specific ways in which female welfare clients are exposed to the disabling effects of welfare professionals. Feminists have done more, however, than simply bring in a gender dimension to existing critiques. They have moved the debate on the Welfare State forward in two crucial respects.

First, they have attempted to develop theories of social conflict which explain why women are *systematically* disadvantaged in society, including in the Welfare State. This has involved exploring the issue of whether men and women, as members of socially constructed gender groups, have conflicting interests.

Second, feminists have exposed the inequalities of power within the home which are key elements in women's oppression. This has led to a broadening of the traditional focus of political concern. Feminists have argued that 'the personal is political' to reinforce the idea that women's liberation depends on changing what have traditionally been thought of as purely private matters. Since the Welfare State plays an important role in structuring personal relationships, feminist goals must necessarily involve a new overall social policy which gives women and men more choices as to how they live their lives.

In this book we will draw together a wide ranging, diverse and substantive body of feminist research and analysis which documents women's inequality within the Welfare State and analyses the ways in which the welfare services reinforce inequalities in other spheres of women's lives such as the workplace. We hope, therefore, that it will be particularly useful to anyone seeking a broad based introduction to a feminist critique of the Welfare State.

However, we sought to do more than simply compile existing feminist writing. Whilst all feminists share certain core assumptions about the disadvantages women suffer, there are equally wide differences between them on many issues. We will be centrally concerned with these debates. This involves comparing and evaluating the alternative and sometimes conflicting perspectives on both the causes of women's subordination within the Welfare State and strategies for change. We will also put forward our own views on the complex relationships between the oppression of women and the power exercised by men, capitalism and the State, and explore certain aspects of women's role within the Welfare State which we believe have been overlooked or under-researched by other writers. We hope, therefore, that this book will not only provide a review of the existing state of play between feminism and welfare but that it will also move that play forward just a little.

Part I:

Feminists and the historical development of the Welfare State

1

Feminism and the Welfare State: the formative years

1 Introduction

What impact did feminism have on the development of the Welfare State? If we were to pose this question to a group of feminists active in today's liberation movement we might expect them to reply that feminism had been marginal to the development of the Welfare State, and as a result the Welfare State in many respects oppresses women. If we had put the same question to a group of feminists in the late 1940s, the years when the Labour Government was giving shape to a comprehensive system of welfare provision, we might have received a rather different answer. Most, although not all, feminists welcomed the post-war welfare reforms as improving women's material position and status in society. In the early 1950s, for example, Vera Brittain, a feminist since her youth in the years around the First World War, argued that the 'women's question' had been transformed into the substance of the Welfare State.

> ... in it women have become ends in themselves and not merely means to the ends of men. The welfare state has been both cause and consequence of the second great change by which women have moved ... from rivalry with men to a new recognition of their unique value as women. (Brittain, 1953, p. 224.)

For Brittain, feminism and the Welfare State were two sides of the same coin. Without the campaigns of the women's movement for the needs of mothers and children to be recognized and for the values of caring to be given social recognition, there would have been no Welfare State. For women, the establishment of the Welfare State was the culmination of their struggle for equality and dignity. Women's needs and interest were no longer ignored in the political system, or treated as the opportunity for jokes and masculine titillation. Women had achieved the right to be treated as equals to men, whilst retaining a sense of their special qualities which had received public recognition in social policies which put need above economic and political power.

In this chapter we shall look at the ideas and activities of feminists during the formative years of the contemporary Welfare State, from the turn of the century to the Second World War. We shall seek to understand how and why their ideas differed from those of feminists today, and what impact they had on the development of social legislation. Did earlier feminists simply not challenge many of the sexist assumptions embodied in social policy? Or did they struggle to change policies, only to be defeated?

2 Early twentieth century feminists

Dale Spender argues in the title of a recent book that *There's Always Been a Women's Movement This Century* (Spender, 1983b). Indeed, there has always been a women's movement, because there have always been organizations of women campaigning to promote women's interests in society. However, many of the older feminists whom Dale Spender interviewed for her book were sympathetic, yet slightly puzzled, or almost shocked by some aspects of today's movement compared with that of their youth. This is hardly surprising, since the two movements differ in a range of ways, in particular, in their understanding of 'women's interests', their methods of organization, the range of women involved.

Early twentieth century feminists were mainly concerned with the *public* sphere, and unlike contemporary feminists, tended to take the private sphere of the home for granted. They concentrated on two types of activity: gaining access for women to education, employment and political influence, and campaigning for public provision of welfare to meet the needs of non-working women. The vast majority of feminists did not see the sexual division of labour in the home as necessarily oppressive, and many glorified women's role as mother.

These campaigning priorities are associated with a second

contrast with the women's movement today, their method of organizing themselves. Almost all the earlier women's groups favoured the traditional pressure-group type of organization which typically had a formal constitution, and elected national or central committee, with quite formal and elaborate rules of procedure. Their activities might include demonstrations, but they concentrated on peaceful persuasion, building alliances with (male) MPs, other organizations and lobbying patiently behind the scenes.

The exception to this generalization is, of course, the militant suffragettes of the Women's Social and Political Union, who broke away from their more staid sisters in the early years of the twentieth century and gradually moved towards a militant campaign beginning with window breaking, and culminating in arson. In the process, they abandoned constitutional organization, for a form of charismatic leadership.

The third difference between past and present is the social composition of the movement. Taken together, women's organizations represented a very wide spectrum from single, middle class career women to working class housewives. The sheer number of women who were members of some women's organization or another is quite striking compared with today. On the other hand, this breadth meant that the organizations might have very different priorities. In particular, the social class division within the movement was very pronounced.

We shall explore these differences further by looking at two strands of feminism active during the first half of the twentieth century, namely liberal feminism and what Banks refers to as 'welfare feminism' (Banks, 1981). Our focus on only these two groups of women is justified by the fact that they encompassed the main women's organizations which campaigned around welfare issues during the years after 1906 when the most important and enduring foundations of today's Welfare State were being laid. A study of their ideas, and their successes and failures should therefore give us important clues as to why the Welfare State developed in ways which contemporary feminists regard as oppressive. We do not pretend to give a comprehensive picture of earlier feminist movements and readers wishing to know more about other strands of feminism should consult the works of historians such as Olive Banks (1981), Sheila Rowbotham (1973a) and Barbara Taylor (1983).

Liberal feminism refers to that strand of feminism which was and indeed still is concerned with ending legal discrimination against women and removing all barriers which prevent their entry into the public sphere on equal terms with men. During the last three decades of the nineteenth century a series of campaigns emerged to improve women's legal and economic position. In particular, women campaigned to remove the legal disabilities of married women which denied them the right to own property, or to take custody of their children after separation or divorce, and which sanctioned a double standard of morality in divorce. They also opened up secondary and higher education to women by establishing women's schools and colleges and gaining women the right to sit for degrees, and to enter certain of the professions which previously barred women from membership. Many of these campaigns were waged by individual women, or small networks rather than by an identifiable movement. The cause which can truly be said to have created a women's *movement* was the campaign for the vote.

The campaign for the vote emerged in the last decades of the nineteenth century and took organizational shape with the formation of the National Union of Women's Suffrage Societies (NUWSS), led by Millicent Garrett Fawcett, in 1897. By the Edwardian period many battles in other spheres were won, or the major breakthrough had been achieved: women could take degrees and practise medicine; married women could own property. The struggle for the vote was to become the cause which, for liberal feminists, dominated all others. Ray Strachey for example, editor of the *Common Cause* the NUWSS newspaper, could write her history of the women's movement up to 1928 (Strachey, 1978) without reference to developments in social policy, despite the fact that, from 1906 onwards, the modern Welfare State was beginning to take shape.

Most liberal feminists concentrated on the issue of the vote because they believed it would give women more political influence. Many also tended not to interest themselves greatly in the extension of social welfare before the First World War because they supported a liberal approach to economic policy which is suspicious of state intervention. Anna Martin, a contributor to *Common Cause* opposed both free school meals and child allowances on the grounds that they would weaken fathers' responsibility to maintain their wives and children and tend to lead to a fall in wages (Martin, 1911). Before we dismiss Martin as reactionary, however, it is worth pointing out that she did not oppose all state intervention – she favoured a minimum wage policy for example – and she accurately reflected some of the views of working class women who also might be suspicious of state intervention:

... the women have a vague dread of being superseded and dethroned. Each of them knows perfectly well that the strength of her position in the home lies in the physical dependence of husband and children upon her, and is suspicious of anything that could tend to undermine it. (Martin, 1911, p. 30.)

After the First World War, attitudes amongst liberal feminists changed. The NUWSS changed its name to the National Union of Societies for Equal Citizenship (NUSEC), and began to campaign for equal rights for women in social and economic matters. From the late 1920s, this shift became more pronounced and feminists such as Eleanor Rathbone began to talk of the 'new feminism' which instead of seeking equality with men, was more concerned with women's specific needs and aspirations (Rathbone 1929). In 1927 NUSEC split on the issue of protective legislation – i.e. laws which limited the hours and type of work in which women could engage. To equal rights feminists, all protective legislation was a form of discrimination against women, whilst the 'new feminists' argued that it should be considered from the point of view of the well-being of the community and whether workers affected supported it. Underlying this split was a deep difference as to the aims of feminism: was it about equal rights, or about welfare issues such as family allowances and birth control. To Rathbone, the older feminists were becoming somewhat irrelevant, whereas to equal rights feminists there was, in the words of Elizabeth Abbott: 'a grave danger of the National Union becoming a society among many for promoting social reforms – instead of a living instrument for the liberation of women'. (NUSEC, 1927, p. 2.)

During the 1930s, NUSEC (from 1932, the National Council for Equal Citizenship) became increasingly absorbed in welfare issues, whilst the liberal feminist approach was kept alive by smaller feminist organizations such as the Women's Freedom League, the Six Point Group and the Open Door Council.

Discussion of the changing attitude of NUSEC brings us to the second strand of feminism, which we describe as 'welfare'. NUSEC moved in this direction in the 1920s but it had existed since the turn of the century as a movement of labour movement women in trade unions and organizations such as the Women's Co-operative Guild formed in 1883 as an offshoot of the co-operative movement. We have described this strand of feminism 'welfare' rather than socialist because of its emphasis on immediate social reform rather than the wider horizons of socialist transformation. Socialist women who were also feminists, such as Sylvia Pankhurst, identified less and less with the women's movement as they became caught up in the wider debates surrounding revolutionary strategy in the aftermath of the Russian Revolution.

Unlike liberal feminists, welfare feminists tended to prioritize the immediate material interests of women over and above abstract notions of equal rights, and were less likely to place gender interests above class interests. This difference of priority could lead to a direct conflict in demands. During the campaigns for the vote, for example, before the First World War, labour women such as Margaret Bondfield and the Women's Co-operative Guild argued against giving women the vote on the same terms as men, on the grounds that the existing franchise for men included a property qualification. Bondfield did not oppose middle class women seeking the vote, but warned: 'don't let them come and tell me that they are working for my class.' (WFL, 1908 p. 15.)

An even deeper division existed in relation to the issue of protective legislation. As a result of such divisions, labour movement feminism remained somewhat separate from the main women's movement before the First World War. In the 1930s however, the increasingly welfarist orientation of NUSEC meant that it often worked closely with the Guild.

Finally, we must mention a whole range of organizations which attempted to draw women into public life through emphasizing the responsibilities of citizenship, in particular the National Council of Women and the local Women's Citizenship Committees. These organizations are perhaps not truly *feminist*, but they played a role in articulating women's interests, and many women who regarded themselves as feminists were active in them. We shall therefore include them in our account.

This review of feminist movements raises a number of points which are relevant to understanding the impact of feminism on the Welfare State before 1945. In the first place, the feminist movement was divided along class lines which weakened its impact on the labour and trade union movement and hence on the Labour Party. The equal rights tradition of feminism could all too easily be dismissed as 'middle class', having little relevance to working class women.

In the second place, the campaign which highlighted women's unequal position in society was the struggle for the vote. This campaign served as a focus for a whole range of women's grievances about their lack of political and economic power, and the way they were treated by men. Once the vote had been won the feminist movement seemed to lose its sense of identity and purpose. The militant suffragettes tended to disappear, or pressed for an equal rights programme which was irrelevant to most women – amongst the key demands of the Women's Freedom League, for example, were women's right to sit in the House of Lords, and the opening of the Consular and Diplomatic Service to women! The constitutionalists became more and more involved in welfare issues, and seemed to lose any specifically *feminist* approach.

The third striking feature of the first generation of feminists is their apparent acceptance of many crucial aspects of the gender system which modern feminists regard as oppressive: in particular their stance towards the family, and sexual norms.

The majority of feminists saw nothing inherently wrong in women being economically dependent on men so long as they received some protection. Many feminists saw the solution to married women's economic vulnerability in wives gaining the legal right to a share of their husband's income. When Ada Nield Chew, a working class socialist feminist argued against this in the *Common Cause* and unequivocally for the right of mothers to work outside the home, the editor felt compelled to publish a disclaimer pointing out that articles represented the views of authors alone. (*Common Cause* 6 March 1914)

Raising the status of motherhood and laying the basis for companionate marriage were central to both strands of feminism. Most feminist organizations had a specific set of demands relating to the status of married women, and in 1938 the Married Women's Association was founded as an offshoot of the Six Point Group with the aim of creating a legal and financial partnership in marriage. This is important when we come to analyse the way a dominant family ideology has come to be embodied in social policy. We cannot argue that it was simply 'foisted' on women: those who took a more radical stance against the sexual division of labour in the home were few and far between.

The acceptance of the ideology of motherhood and the family often took on a nationalist and eugenic slant. Margaret Bondfield, a labour movement woman argued that:
'The nurture of children is a *race* matter, a question in which the strength and survival of the community is involved, and in which women must take the leading part assigned them by nature.'
(Bondfield, 1949, p. 135 emphasis in original.)

Similarly, feminists generally adopted a conventional attitude towards sex morals. In part this was a question of respectability:

9

at a time when women were judged by their sexual probity, any scandal might have impeded the reforms in other areas which women achieved. Hence, the NUWSS distanced itself from Josephine Butler's campaigns against the state regulation of prostitution, not because suffragist women were unsympathetic, but because they feared the taint of scandal. More fundamentally, however, feminist women tended to adopt a view of women as victims of a predatory male sexuality. The attack on the double standard was essentially a demand that men live up to the standard of morality they set for women rather than an argument for sexual freedom for women. As a result, feminists were ambivalent towards issues such as birth control and only supported the birth control campaign after the First World War. Even then, it was pursued within a social democratic discourse of 'hardship to mothers' resulting from unnecessary pregnancies. Single women were seen by the majority of feminists as having no choice but to remain celibate.

All these factors shaped the nature and extent of feminism's impact on the emerging Welfare State. In the next section, we shall look in more detail at the main feminist campaigns around welfare in the years prior to the Second World War.

3 Feminist campaigns

Feminists campaigned around many issues during the years between 1906 and 1939. Three issues, however, dominated others: the inclusion of women in the developing system of national insurance; economic assistance to mothers through maternity benefits and some form of family allowances; and finally, maternal and child health. We shall look at the aims and impact of feminists in these three areas.

The introduction of national insurance in 1911 raised a whole range of issues concerning women's position in the social security system. In the first place, the very concept of insurance disadvantages women who give up work to have children and are therefore unable to build up sufficient contributions to receive adequate benefits in their own right.

Second, however, the original Act and much subsequent legislation have compounded this disadvantage by treating men and women workers differently, in particular by requiring women to pay lower contributions and in return paying considerably reduced benefits.

By 1911, the suffrage societies were well organized, and in their newspapers *Common Cause* and *Votes for Women* they highlighted the inequalities and injustices in the scheme. There is a sense, however, in which their concerns about national insurance were subordinate to the demand for the vote. For example, a meeting in July 1911 protested against the treatment of women in the Bill but concluded that:

> they regard the blindness of the Bill to the interests of women as an instance of that political negligence which is always the lot of the unenfranchised, and they urge upon the Government to give the earliest possible facilities next year for the passing of the Women's Suffrage Conciliation Bill. (*Common Cause* 20 July 1911, p. 270.)

The more detailed pressure group work seems to have been undertaken by the National Council of Women, a broad, umbrella body for women's organizations, which emphasized 'social responsibility' and 'citizenship' as much as feminism. The NCW set up a Special Committee to Safeguard Women's Interests under the National Insurance Bill amongst whose forty-two members, were twelve MPs. The NCW concentrated on specific injustices, in response to which the Government made some concessions. However, the major discriminatory features of the 1911 Act remained firmly entrenched. In particular, women could not become voluntary contributors if they gave up paid work; men and women's contributions and benefits were unequal; and maternity grant was made the property of the father rather than the mother. This last provision was reversed in 1913 after a campaign spearheaded by the Women's Co-operative Guild.

National Insurance was regarded as revolutionary because it introduced benefits as of right based on a contractual relationship, rather than discretionary assistance involving tests of both means and morals. As far as married women were concerned, however, this right was never unambiguously conceded, and in practice married women often had to fulfil extra conditions before they were awarded benefit. In 1921 a clause was introduced requiring claimants to prove that they were 'genuinely seeking work.' Deacon (1976) observes that this excited relatively little opposition from the labour movement because it was mainly used against married women. In 1931, a bill to deal with certain 'anomalies' was piloted through the House of Commons by Margaret Bondfield, the first woman cabinet minister. The subsequent Act required married women to 'prove' that they had not abandoned insurable employment and could reasonably expect to find such work in their district. Between October and December 1931, 38 per cent of claims by married women were disallowed under the new regulations (Deacon, 1976).

Despite concern expressed at such inequities, only the smaller, liberal feminist organizations continued to campaign for the principle of equality in social insurance. The main focus of campaigning by the largest feminist organizations was economic assistance to mothers, and maternal and child health. The major role was played by the Women's Co-operative Guild, which had consistently made social need rather than equality its platform, and NUSEC which, under Eleanor Rathbone's presidency, had moved away from the demand for equal rights in favour of prioritizing the needs of mothers and children.

The campaign for the endowment of motherhood is particularly associated with the name of Eleanor Rathbone, and the Family Endowment Society she founded in 1917. The feminist credentials of this campaign did not simply lie in the fact that its aim was to redistribute income to women. Rathbone and others saw family allowances as indispensable in the fight for equal pay – they were the irrefutable answer to the male assertion that they needed a 'family wage'. This view was not, however, supported by all feminists – and many non-feminists supported family allowances for eugenic reasons. These criss-crossing debates were reflected in a gradual shift in the FES away from any feminist identity as it attempted to gain official support. By 1927, only five on the fifteen person executive were feminists, and the FES seems to have approached the issue of the relationship between endowment and wages from a *class* rather than a feminist perspective. In particular, in 1925, the FES gave evidence to the Samuel Commission on the Mining Industry, and argued that family allowances would provide the means to cut wages without causing hardship to workers (Macnicol, 1980). Instead of the redistributive consequences of family allowances being in favour of women, they were thus to favour capital at the expense of labour. In the next section we shall see how the introduction of family allowances in 1945 had less to do with feminism and the needs of women, than governmental concern about inflation and a falling birthrate.

The third area of feminist campaigning centred on maternal health and infant welfare. Once again, the Women's Co-operative Guild and later NUSEC played a central role. Unlike more middle-class, liberal feminist organizations, the WCG had its roots firmly planted in the experience of ordinary working-class women. It was these experiences which formed the basis of their demands for a national maternity service. In 1914, the Guild sent a questionnaire to their members asking them to give their experiences of maternity. The replies, giving a graphic picture of ill-health and exhaustion, were published the following year, and two editions were sold out within two months (Re-published as Davies, 1978). Women's groups were pushing an already open door in so far as the State also was concerned about the high levels of infant and maternal mortality. We have already seen, however, in relation to maternity grant how official concern could lead to the introduction of policies which ignored women's needs and rights, and this tension continued to exist during the inter-war years.

In 1918, the Maternal and Child Welfare Act required local authorities to set up maternal and child welfare committees, and this gave further impetus to organizations such as the WCG who attempted to get women councillors onto the committees. Throughout the inter-war years the Guild campaigned for more hospital provisions for confinements, home helps, and municipal mother and infant centres - popular with mothers - rather than voluntary run 'schools for mothers' and health visitors which were experienced by many mothers as imposition and social control. In the 1930s both the WCG and NUSEC campaigned around issues from milk to dependents' benefits in social insurance through an organization known as the Children's Minimum Council (Gaffin and Thoms, 1903).

Although birth control is seen today as an aspect of sexual freedom, in the inter-war years many women supported contraceptive rights as part of their campaigns around maternal health. Groups of women encountered intense hostility when they opened birth control clinics, and it is perhaps not surprising that in their efforts to make birth control more respectable they emphasized the needs of mothers rather than *all* women. Some women went further, however, in seeing birth control as playing a eugenic role in improving the racial stock (Lewis, 1980). Once again middle class women incorporated class and imperialist ideologies into their feminism.

Considerable improvements were registered in maternal and child welfare during the inter-war period. In 1918, many local authorities did not know what an ante-natal clinic was, but by 1937 there were 1,307 in existence; hospital births rose from 1 per cent in 1910–14 to 17 per cent in 1935–9; maternal mortality, which had remained stubbornly high, and even increased until the mid-1930s, fell dramatically in the final years of the decade. The form of many policies reflected official concern about the state of the population and professional interests as much as the needs of women, leaving Lewis pondering the unanswerable question of: 'whether the decrease in infant mortality could or should be weighed against a subtle strengthening of the ideology of motherhood, or better medical care in childbirth against the loss of control by women over its management.' (Lewis, 1980, p. 21.)

One final area of women's concern which deserves a brief mention is that of housing policy. This is an interesting case study since it was an area of policy officially defined as in women's sphere of interest. Thus during the First World War, the Ministry of Reconstruction appointed a Women's Housing Sub-Committee to advise on the design of houses. The Sub-Committee's report was in certain respects quite radical, going beyond house design to include suggestions for communal laundry services, cheap restaurants and communal holiday homes (Ministry of Reconstruction, 1919). After the war, local authorities were encouraged to set up their own women's sub-committees. Experience in Manchester suggests that they channelled women's energies into struggling to make marginal adjustments to architectural designs drawn up by men – who resisted even the modest suggestion that windows be designed with opening toplights to improve ventilation! Such was the strength of 'civic responsibility' experienced by women's organizations at the time, that in Manchester they continued to battle on until they were officially dissolved in 1944. (Minutes of the Women's Housing Advisory Committee, Manchester.)

The inter-war years tend to be regarded as the doldrums both for feminism and the development of social policy. In retrospect, the period can be seen as one in which major improvements in women's material position were recorded: by 1939 most women were included within the scope of national insurance, widows' pensions had been introduced, and the number of maternity and child welfare centres had increased greatly. Nevertheless, in the process, a specifically *feminist* orientation seems to have been lost. We shall now see how well- or ill-equipped the feminist movement was to influence the post-war reconstruction of the Welfare State.

4 Feminists and 1945

The Second World War is often seen as having had a profound influence on British social life and social policy. Titmuss, for example, argues that social change is accelerated by a number of factors subsumed under the concept of 'total war': the state requires the involvement of the whole population and as a result takes greater responsibility for its health and welfare; the position of subordinate groups is strengthened and promises of post-war social reform become a necessary means of engaging popular support.

This analysis is helpful in explaining the strengthening of the labour movement during the war and the impetus to social democratic welfare reforms immediately afterwards. When we turn to examine the position of women, however, the picture becomes more complicated. The State needed women's labour power and women's support every bit as much as it needed men's. This in turn stirred women into action to demand real changes in their social position. Little in terms of lasting change was achieved, however, as neither the labour movement nor the political parties were prepared to give women their share of the fruits of sacrifice. We must modify Titmuss' thesis of total war: such wars create the conditions in which state aims coincide to some extent with those of subordinate groups and their position is temporarily improved. However, *lasting* change depends on a fundamental change in the balance of forces – on struggles whose outcome is by no means a foregone conclusion.

During the Second World War women were brought into war-related activities in a wide range of areas, both in the women's services, in civil defence work and in industry. Both military and industrial conscription were introduced. This involvement raised two burning issues for women: equal pay and equal compensation for war-related injuries. On the first issue, the feminist movement achieved little. The Government specifically refused to concede equal pay for women subject to industrial conscription, and in this the Conservative dominated coalition was backed by Labour leaders such as Bevin, who warned that, if the question of equal pay were raised at all: '. . . industrial peace might be endangered for the rest of the war.' (Quoted in Smith, 1981 p. 652.)

When Conservative MP Thelma Cazalet Keir introduced an amendment to the 1944 Education Act granting teachers equal pay, Churchill, again with Bevin's backing, made the issue one of confidence in the Government. In the face of such determined and united opposition to women's claims little was achieved.

The issue of equal compensation for war-related injuries, however, was a different story. A wide range of women's organizations came together to fight against the unequal provisions of the 1939 Personal Injuries (Emergency Provisions) Act. The campaign lasted several years, the major opposition coming from those such as Bevin and Churchill who feared that equal compensation would open the door to equal pay. In the event, this was avoided by the setting up of a Select Committee whose terms of reference specifically excluded any discussion of equal pay (Smith, 1981). In April 1943, the Government conceded the women's demands.

Another issue where there had traditionally been a conflict between the interests of women and male trade unionists had been that of family allowances which welfare feminists had been demanding for two decades or more. During the war, labour movement suspicions were gradually dissipated and Macnicol (1980) argues that the largely negative official view changed as the government realized that family allowances would provide a useful tool in its attempt to moderate wage demands. Macnicol largely writes off feminist pressure as having had any influence on the decision to introduce legislation in 1945. Whilst it is undoubtedly true that the male dominated parliament and civil service was primarily concerned with problems of economic management rather than women's needs, it is nevertheless noteworthy that the initial proposal for payment to the father as the 'normal household head' was overturned by a free vote in Parliament. Perhaps, therefore, Macnicol is too harsh in writing feminists' campaigns completely off the agenda.

When we come to look at the debates surrounding the most important war-time social policy document, the Beveridge Report, we find that the women's movement was lively and vibrant compared with the 1930s, but that whilst it could achieve some success on limited and specific objectives, it was not strong enough to secure more fundamental change.

A number of women's organizations gave evidence to the Beveridge Report, notably the Married Women's Association, the National Council of Women, the Six Point Group, the Women's Co-operative Guild, and the Women's Freedom League. Asked specifically to comment on the 'problem' of the insurance of the married woman, the NCW was firm that her marital status should be no concern of the insurance administrators. Men and women should be treated equally, paying equal contributions for equal benefits (*Social Insurance and Allied Services: Memoranda from Organisations*, 1942). Beveridge, however, had his own ideas, and in his report placed married women in a special insurance category of their own. Married women workers could choose whether to pay full insurance stamps or be exempt. In the former case, they still paid less than men, on the grounds that the male stamp financed benefits for dependants, and received lower rates of unemployment and disability benefit.

Married women who gave up paid work on marriage were to lose their entitlement to any benefits based on contributions made before marriage, receiving in return a marriage grant by way of compensation.

The Beveridge Report excited angry reactions from many feminists. The most scathing indictments come from a pamphlet published by two women associated with the Open Door Council (Abbot and Bompas, 1943). They condemn the idea of the marriage grant as 'selling a birthright for a mess of pottage' (p. 6), and argue for all women to have an independent insured status, paying the same contributions and receiving the same benefits as men. This argument was taken up by the Six Point Group and in 1944 twelve women's organizations united in a deputation to the Government.

Against this feminist viewpoint, many women welcomed the Beveridge Report. This was not simply because it was 'better than nothing'. Many women saw the Report as *improving* the status of housewives. One of the most famous passages of the Beveridge Report is that where he argues: 'the great majority of married women must be regarded as occupied on work which is vital though unpaid, without which their husbands could not do their paid work and without which the nation could not continue.' (*Social Insurance and Allied Services: Report by Sir William Beveridge*, para. 107 p. 49.)

This passage appears in the section where Beveridge argues that housewives have received insufficient recognition under existing insurance schemes. Whilst much of Beveridge's argument is rhetoric which fails to hide the reality of the dependent status of housewives under the scheme, many women nevertheless saw it as an advance in that it recognized the existence of housewives and gave them legal status. Thus Brittain argued that the Report recognized 'home-makers' for the first time, and in the parliamentary debate on the Report Mrs Cazalet Keir MP who was a leading figure in the Equal Pay Campaign Committee, argued that: 'Everybody, I think, welcomes in the Beveridge Report the new economic status which has been given to the housewife. At last it is recognized as equal to that of any profession.' (Hansard, 16 February 1943 para 1793.)

None of the four women speakers in the debate echoed any of the feminist criticisms discussed earlier. Thus post-war social policy continued very much in the tradition set in the inter-war years – improvements in material well-being were achieved through the extension of health services, social insurance, and family allowances. However, these policies were cast within a framework of married women's assumed dependence on men which today's feminists regard as at the heart of women's oppression.

Conclusion

What lessons can we learn from the activities of the women's movement up to the Second World War? In the first place, the feminist movement was much broader in its social base than it is today. It was able to appeal to a wide range of ordinary women, and the sheer range of organizations in existence, and the size of their memberships is quite striking in comparison with the movement today. Apart from the militant suffragettes, women's organizations adopted the traditional pressure-group style of organization with formal structures and elected committees and officers. They can be described as reformist in that they were centred on a specific list of potentially winnable demands, and tended to lack any wider theory of women's oppression, or aspirations towards fundamental social change.

The strength of this approach lay in the way it permitted the building of a broad coalition of forces which could have an impact on particular policies. At local level, the network of women's committees enabled women to press for extensions to welfare services provided by local authorities. As a result, women's organizations were able to modify the masculinist orientation of much social policy, and to see welfare services which enhanced women's health and well-being improved. In the process, however, a specifically *feminist* approach seems to have been lost.

Only a few equal rights feminists continued to insist that equality was the key issue, and that women should reject paternalistic protection. Abbot and Bompas, for example, criticized the Beveridge Report for displaying: 'mistaken benevolence from which perhaps more than anything else women need to be emancipated before they can take their place as partners in marriage and work.' (Abbot and Bompas 1943 p. 20.)

We have seen, however, that their voice was lost in a deluge of support for the Report. During most of the inter-war years, the welfare strand of feminism was dominant. Feminists concentrated on the needs of mothers because their needs were indeed greatest. However, in doing so they reinforced the equation women = mother, which underpins the idea that women should be economically dependent on men, and that motherhood is their vocation to the exclusion of paid work.

Although the women's movement straddled all social classes, the organizations themselves were deeply divided along class lines, a factor which weakened its impact on the labour movement and hence on social policy, particularly in the period during and after the Second World War. Those who supported a feminism based on women's interests as a sex, and wanted to promote equality with men rather than simply improve women's material position, tended to be middle and upper class. Welfare feminists were divided between the mainly middle-class women of NUSEC who had their origins in the suffrage movement, and the labour movement women of the Women's Co-operative Guild, who had never seen the suffrage issue as of particular importance. Finally, there were many working class women in the trade union movement who remained outside the sphere of women's organizations altogether, and placed their allegiance to the male labour movement above any identification with women's organizations.

This division was shown up in a glaring way during the Second World War, when feminist organizations took on renewed life and many working women were taking a more militant stance on equal pay. In 1944, an Equal Pay Campaign Committee was set up with representatives from 100 women's organizations with a combined membership of no less than four million women. This impressive support remained classbound, however. The Labour Party's women's advisory body declined to be involved and the Committee campaigned separately from trade unions in the civil service who were also taking the issue up (Smith, 1981). Whilst men in the trade union movement showed little sympathy for feminism, an equally deep cleft seems to have existed between many women trade unionists and feminists.

If we are to draw any overall lessons from a review of the period, they might perhaps be the following. In the first place, our earlier sisters showed that it is possible to build a much broader movement than we have achieved today. Whilst feminist consciousness is widespread amongst women today, this is not reflected in active involvement in feminist politics. The inter-war feminists also had a better grasp of the need to relate to the concrete needs of ordinary women, and how to campaign for specific changes which can be won. They differed from us in their concentration on 'bread and butter' issues, and their use of more structured forms of organizations. Perhaps today when feminists lament the narrow base of the movement or ponder whether the emphasis on loose organizations has produced a new 'tyranny of structurelessness' they may find things to learn from earlier feminists.

Second, however, in promoting the immediate interests of women, longer term goals for women, such as greater autonomy from men, a widening of choices and greater power in society, tended to get lost. In later chapters we shall argue that today's socialist–feminist analysis, an approach which did not really exist in the pre-war period, offers the most fruitful way to combine the struggle for short term material gains with a broader perspective on gender relations.

2

Women pioneers in welfare work

1 Introduction

In this chapter we shall look at the historical role of women in welfare work: in particular medicine, nursing, housing management, social work and health visiting. The development of the Welfare State laid the basis for the growth of the medical profession, the expansion and upgrading of nursing work, and the development of new 'women's' occupations such as social work, housing management and health visiting.

The study of these professions and semi-professions is important to us for two reasons. First, with medicine which already existed as a male profession as the exception, women played an important role in the development of these areas of work and formed the majority of workers within them. Second, welfare professions are the main avenues for educated women into higher status, better paid areas of work.

In the case of medicine, we shall document women's fight to enter a profession controlled by men who displayed an almost unbelievable degree of misogyny when faced with the prospect of medicine ceasing to be an exclusively male preserve. In the case of nursing, housing management, social work and health visiting, we shall see how women attempted to develop authentic areas of women's work, and in so doing were involved in the creation of those professions in their modern form. This came about in two ways. In the first place, women's involvement in philanthropy led to the development of new professions. These were regarded as women's work because they involved intervention in the home, which was regarded as women's sphere, and because the main contact in the home was the housewife. A woman visitor would, it was thought, establish a better relationship with her, and give both practical advice and an element of befriending.

The second contribution of women was to upgrade and revolutionize an existing area of women's work, nursing. Whilst the moral and psychological motivation for women to engage in nursing was similar to that behind philanthropy, nursing differed in two ways. First, it was located in public institutions – hospitals and workhouses – rather than touching on the home. This meant that, second, the rationale for it being women's work was slightly different. Originally nurses were women because the job was seen as akin to domestic work. After the upgrading of nursing, the rationale shifted to women's aptitude for caring.

The development of women's professions is highly ambiguous for feminists. On the one hand, the idea of 'women's work' gave them an impetus to press for greater opportunities for women. It also enabled women to highlight the contribution they could make as *women* to the development of social services. On the other hand, in so doing they could reinforce dominant ideologies which trapped women in particular gender roles.

In examining this history we are seeking to understand the terms on which women moved out of the home and into the public sphere. Ehrenreich and English (1979) argue that women faced two possible models for this: the romantic model which accepts the traditional gender roles, with their link between women and the home, and the rationalist, which seeks access to education and work on the same terms as men. We shall see in the remainder of this chapter which models women chose.

2 Women and medicine: storming male bastions

Feminist historians suggest that the women who fought to become fully qualified doctors during the second half of the nineteenth century were not so much breaking new ground, as reclaiming women's rightful heritage as healers. According to Ehrenreich and English 'For centuries women were doctors without degrees, barred from books and lectures, learning from each other and passing on experience from neighbour to neighbour and mother to daughter.' (Ehrenreich and English, 1973 (b), p. 3.) Ehrenreich and English claim that until the eighteenth century all forms of healing including pharmacy, childbirth, abortions and even primitive forms of surgery, were mainly women's work. As medicine became professionalized, however, women were gradually excluded. They remained as informal carers, and in the then untrained work of midwifery but the medical *profession* was, by the mid-nineteenth century, an exclusively male preserve, which barred women from entry through legal restrictions on access to education and to the medical register.

Women's struggles to enter medicine can be seen as part of a wider campaign to open educational opportunities for women. Feminists such as Emily Davies who founded Girton College Cambridge, believed that women had to demonstrate their abilities through competing in examinations on the same terms as men. All faced opposition from men although perhaps few had to go through the ordeals which were to meet women pursuing a medical education.

In 1869 Sophia Jex-Blake and several other women students were pelted with rotten vegetables by male medical students at Edinburgh University who objected to these women taking a medical examination. This incident was later referred to as a 'riot' by the local press. Subsequently the women were harassed in the streets by groups of hostile students who shouted 'obscene' anatomical terms at them – terms which the female medical students fully understood but which the police failed to recognize as obscenities. It requires little imagination to appreciate the intimidatory effect such tactics must have had on well brought up Victorian ladies.

The 'logical' arguments put forward by male doctors in their attempt to prevent these women from obtaining medical degrees and then gaining postgraduate experience were many and varied. A very popular argument was that higher education of any sort would endanger women's health, particularly their reproductive capacities. On the other hand some opponents stressed that they were most concerned about their patients' welfare. Dr Horatio Storer, for example, was particularly concerned about the safety of patients treated by women doctors during 'their often infirmity' (i.e. periods) since at this time, Storer claimed, many women went temporarily insane (Quoted in Walsh, 1977 p. 111). A third popular argument used against letting women into medical schools in the late nineteenth century was that co-educational classes in subjects such as anatomy would be indecent. For example, Professor Laycock of Edinburgh University told Sophia Jex-Blake that he 'could not imagine any decent woman wishing to study medicine' while 'as for any lady that was out of the question'. Some male lecturers, however, were happy to teach women in separate classes as long as they received extra remuneration for their extra work (Jex-Blake, 1886).

Behind these overt objections to women training as doctors lay rather less pure motives for keeping women out of the medical profession. Walsh emphasizes the pecuniary considerations which lay behind many male doctors' fears of an influx of women into their lucrative fields of practice – particularly gynaecology and obstetrics. Doctors specializing in female complaints were particularly worried that their private female patients would choose a woman doctor in order to avoid the embarrassment of revealing their bodies to a male doctor. This particular worry was probably well founded. According to Sophia Jex-Blake, speaking from considerable personal experience, even 'rough women of a very poor class' refrained from seeking medical help for certain medical conditions because they could not bring themselves to see 'a man with such a trouble' whilst other women patients told her 'It's so nice isn't it, to be able at last to ask ladies about such things?' (Jex-Blake, 1886, p 44.)

The idea that the objections to women becoming doctors were based primarily on economic considerations is by no means a modern interpretation of distant events. All those caught up in the controversy over women studying medicine at Edinburgh in the 1870s openly debated the extent to which male doctors were concerned about their livelihoods. A certain Dr Phin, for example, argued that if women were allowed to train as doctors they would 'snatch the bread from the mouths of poor practitioners' (Jex-Blake, 1886). Money was by no means the only covert motive behind the male backlash against women doctors. Walsh argues that many doctors had typically Victorian attitudes towards male and female roles and were upset and emotionally threatened by the rise of independent career-minded Victorian women. According to Walsh: 'male physicians uneasily contemplating the female challenge in their own field, saw in women doctors something more than professional competitors. Women were competing for the power that had been a man's right in a patriarchal society.' (Walsh, 1977, p. 141.)

Sophia Jex-Blake's own account of the opposition to her studying medicine at Edinburgh suggests yet another motive behind male lecturers and students' objections to women joining their classes. Her account makes it clear that hitherto medical schools had been run on the lines of all male clubs where men could let their hair down and generally enjoy themselves in rather crude ways.

Despite the many overt and covert objections which constituted a concerted, often viscous, campaign against women entering medicine in the late nineteenth century, these women – supported by a strong women's movement and, to be fair, by a number of sympathetic male doctors, professors and medical students – made significant advances towards opening the medical profession to particularly able and strong willed women. In 1865 Elizabeth Garrett became the first woman doctor to qualify by passing the examination of the Society of Apothecaries who, under their existing rules, remained the only examining board which could not legally exclude women examinees. After her success the society changed its rules so that no further women could find their way into the profession. Nevertheless, under the impact of campaigns by women such as Sophia Jex-Blake and Elizabeth Garrett (who on marriage took the name Anderson) and sympathetic male MPs, Parliament passed the 1876 Medical Act which enabled all examining boards to admit women. By then the London School of Medicine for Women had been founded through the efforts of Sophia Jex-Blake in particular, and by 1900 there were 258 practising women doctors in England.

Today women form around a quarter of members of the British Medical Association and there are almost as many women medical students as men. Women doctors tend, however, to remain concentrated in the least prestigious areas – community health services and general practice.

Besides providing employment opportunities for women, the women pioneers also provided choice for women patients. In 1866 Elizabeth Garrett founded the St Mary's Dispensary for Women in London, which proved to be immensely popular with women patients and eventually grew to be the Elizabeth Garrett Anderson Hospital for Women which continues to exist today because contemporary feminists have fought to save it from closure.

The early pioneers suffered immense discrimination because of their sex, and as a result tended to identify with the feminist movement. Today, when there are far more women doctors, we cannot assume a link with feminism or even necessarily a more sympathetic understanding of women's problems and needs. Nevertheless, there have always been feminist doctors who have joined with other women to push forward the frontiers of the welfare state – whether in birth control clinics in the 1920s or well-women clinics in the 1980s.

3 Fit work for women – nursing

Nursing as an occupation developed with the wave of hospital building that occurred during the first half of the nineteenth century. The early nurses were untrained working class women whose role was that of institutional domestic: ' "Nurses" said a doctor "were in the position of housemaids and needed only the simplest instructions." ' (Baly, 1973, p. 72.)

It was the nursing reform movement pioneered by Florence Nightingale which raised the status of nursing and forged a new profession for women. Florence Nightingale became famous in her day for her work among soldiers during the Crimean War. On her return, her popularity and support from influential political figures enabled her to establish the Nightingale School for Nurses despite the opposition of many doctors who still regarded nurses as domestic workers. The basis of nursing training was the unification of the science of hygiene with the practical tasks of physical care and domestic work. Trained nurses were to go out to other hospitals, where the low standards of the pre-Nightingale era prevailed, and institute sweeping reforms, thus generally raising nursing standards. The means to achieve such reform was the power of the matron, who would hold absolute authority over all nursing staff. In Nightingale's words, her aim was: 'to take all power over the nursing out of the hands of men and put it into the hands of one female trained head and make her responsible for everything.' (Quoted in Carpenter, 1977 p. 167.)

This stress on female power might seem to cast Nightingale as a feminist. She was however primarily interested in action and problem-solving rather than abstract notions of women's rights. Hence, her distaste for feminist writings and criticism of middle class women's idleness lead some to see her as 'no feminist' (Baly, 1973), whilst Dale Spender can nevertheless argue that Nightingale was uninterested in issues such as the vote simply because she saw them as too limited compared with the truly radical reforms that would be needed to challenge women's subordination (Spender, 1983a).

Nightingale's 'true' beliefs are perhaps not important. What is important from the point of view of later developments, is that Nightingale was prepared to use whatever means were at her disposal to get her ideas put into practice, and that this involved accommodation to the class and gender hierarchy of the hospitals and of society. When she returned from the Crimea, Nightingale became a 'legend in her own lifetime'. She might have been tough and domineering, but the public only wanted to know about the 'lady with the lamp'. This legend:

> ... epitomized what the Victorians believed to be the ideal relationship between man and woman. ... The woman was hard-working and gentle; furthermore, she reached a final fulfilment and happiness in a life of service, offering herself wholly to caring for the male. (Boyd, 1982, p. 187.)

Initially many doctors were suspicious of the trained nurses, but gradually, hospital consultants realized that the nurses could be a great help to them. Hospitals were changing from little more than storehouses for the sick to places of *cure*. If consultants could delegate routine care to trained nurses, thus improving the rate of patient recovery, their own position would be enhanced. Furthermore, at a time when women were pressing to be admitted to medical schools, it was most convenient to have an area of medical work where women did not compete with men. In 1871, a popular monthly magazine included the following:

> Waiving the question whether women might or might not be made capable, with man's advantage of doing man's work, it surely will not be denied that a sphere of action would be preferable in which she did not have to compete with him, but in which her own peculiar endowments would give her a special advantage. And here is an opportunity for showing how a woman's work may complement man's in the true order of nature. Where does the character of the 'helpmeet' come out so strikingly as in the sickroom, where the quick eye, the soft hand, the light step, and the ready ear, second the wisdom of the physician, and execute his will better than he himself could have imagined. (Quoted in Abel-Smith, 1960 p. 18.)

The Nightingale approach accommodated itself to patriarchal structures in other ways. In attempting to raise the status of the profession Nightingale wished to attract upper- and middle-class girls, who were seeking a purpose in life rather than financial reward. At a time when a woman's reputation in whatever she did was judged by the yardstick of her sexual propriety, it was crucial that 'no breath of scandal could assail the Nightingale ladies' (Baly, 1973 p. 73). Hence, Nightingale introduced the innovation of the nurse's home where anxious fathers could be assured that their daughters would be supervised, and engage in only ladylike pursuits.

This attitude to morality was not merely a pragmatic response to the social climate. The Nightingale system represents the 'martinet' tradition of female authority. The matron was supreme, and her subordinates had to give her unquestioning obedience. Thus personality was seen to be as important as book learning – but the personality traits seen as desirable were as much to do with morality and willingness to accept authority, as aptitude for caring for sick people.

This austere and repressive régime was obviously detrimental to the lives of many women nurses. However, the monumental effort to raise the status of the profession did pay off, and in 1919 the registration of the nursing profession was introduced. This process of professionalization took place against the background of the growing liberal feminist movement described in chapter 1. Mrs Fenwick of the Royal British Nursing Association which strongly favoured registration, argued that 'The nurse question is the woman question' (Quoted in Abel-Smith 1960 p. 64).

Whilst the status of nursing was enhanced, 'lady nurses' tended to replace the working class women who made up the untrained nurses. This new status did not bring corresponding financial reward: nursing was seen as a vocation, which legitimated the low pay and restrictive conditions which have characterized nursing ever since.

These characteristics of nursing, which were so detrimental to women who formed the overwhelming majority of nurses, were supported by the matrons, intent on preserving their occupational identity (Carpenter, 1977). Matrons had an interest in legitimating the idea of a female occupation and female authority as embodying a unique disciplinary régime. Within nursing there was a consistent suspicion of male nurses who might have introduced a very different set of ideologies into the profession, and would certainly have given higher priority to issues such as pay and conditions. When nursing registration was introduced in 1919, men were barred from the general register.

During the period after the Second World War, the expansion of the National Health Service increased the demand for nurses, whilst social change, such as the rise in the percentage of women marrying and the lowering of the age of marriage, increased 'wastage' in the profession. The shortage of nursing staff became an issue, and the martinet régime of the matrons was seen as contributing to the problems. At the same time, developments in clinical medicine, and changes in the profile of patients in hospital were leading to a diversification of nursing work. These various forces at work created 'a disequilibrium in the delicate balance of forces which had maintained the occupational infrastructure for so long.' (Carpenter, 1977, p. 173.)

The solution to these various difficulties was sought in the 'professional managerial' model of management imported from industry. A major reorganization of hospital management was inaugurated in the wake of the Salmon Report of 1966, and the unitary management by the matron was replaced by an elongated management structure involving a series of administrative grades. As in social work, the shift towards a managerial model has also led to a change in the ratios of men and women in the profession, with male nurses gaining a disproportionate number of administrative posts.

4 Women, philanthropy and the new professions

Housing management, social work and health visiting all developed out of voluntary work in which women played a dominant role. Prochaska cites a survey carried out in 1893 which referred to about half a million women involved 'continuously and semi-professionally' in philanthropy, and another 20,000 acting as paid officials of charity. (Prochaska, 1980, p. 224.) These figures do not include the tens of thousands who were involved in lesser ways, collecting money or distributing tracts to the poor in their homes. The enormous scale of this involvement was the result of a number of social changes. The middle-class Victorian housewife had time on her hands since she did not work outside the home, and most domestic work was undertaken by servants. Women greatly outnumbered men in the population, leaving many women with little chance of marriage. If they could rely on a private income, they too were seeking a role in society. Both groups turned to philanthropy because of the prevailing moral climate, influenced as it was by an evangelical revival, and because of the absence of other outlets in public life.

A small group of women were not content with a 'Lady Bountiful' role, and used their base in voluntary work to carve out new areas of women's work. Their link with feminism is ambiguous. Their emphasis on solving immediate problems, and their self-sacrificing approach to their work, meant that they were unlikely to be found amongst the ranks of feminist campaigners. Indeed Octavia Hill, the founder of housing management, opposed women's suffrage on the grounds that it would divert women from their true vocation: social reform through local government.

On the other hand, there are links with feminism on a number of levels. The growth of women's public role complemented feminist demands for improved education for girls, and Octavia Hill for example was involved in the education movement. Welfare feminists too saw women workers as humanizing welfare services, and pressed for their employment in the emerging social services.

(i) Housing management

We shall begin this review of women's role in welfare state professions by looking at the case of housing management, since more than any others, it possessed the characteristics of being initiated by a woman, of being promoted as a women's profession, embodying feminine characteristics, which were, however, eventually eclipsed by the development of a 'masculine' orientation. This struggle between 'feminine' and 'masculine' principles is particularly interesting. Women clearly possessed ideas as to how housing should be organized which differed from those of their male contemporaries. These ideas were based very much on women's experience rather than from any specifically *feminist* analysis. Nevertheless some would argue that this experience in itself tends to be progressive – women's approach being somehow naturally less hierarchical and professionalized for example. This issue clearly has relevance to contemporary debates about whether an increase in women welfare providers plays any role in making services more responsive to women's needs.

The development of housing management is associated with the name of Octavia Hill, who began her work in 1864 when she purchased property in London with financial backing from John Ruskin. Her aim was to improve the housing conditions of the poorest class of the population who earned too little to afford the rents charged by the philanthropic housing trusts. Her methods were firmly rooted in Victorian political and moral economy. She saw the poor as victims of their own moral weakness, and referred to them as the 'destructive and criminal classes' as opposed to the 'labouring poor'.

Her methods involving buying up the tenements and courts in which the very poor lived, and instituting a régime of housing management which would ensure their moral and material improvement. As she made clear in her evidence to the Royal Commission for Inquiring into the Housing of the Working

Classes: 'They must be trained' (1885, paragraph 8864). In particular, each tenant's rent and the outgoing on their home was accounted for separately, and repairs and improvements were carried out in proportion to improvements in the tenants' standard of behaviour. To be effective, such a system depended on a rigorous monitoring of tenants' behaviour by a band of volunteer lady rent collectors, supplemented where necessary by information gleaned from authority figures in the local community, such as clergymen.

The needs of the 'labouring poor' she believed could be met by the traditional philanthropic housing trusts so long as costs were pared to a minimum. In practice, this meant building working class tenements of a spartan kind. For example, individual water supplies to each flat were an unnecessary luxury: 'If you have water on every floor that is quite sufficient for working people. It is no hardship to carry a pail of water along a flat surface.' (Royal Commission for Inquiring into the Housing of the Working Classes, 1885 para 8852.)

Octavia Hill opposed state subsidies to housing in any form whatsoever, believing that they were unnecessary, and would tend to lead to a fall in wages and to discourage private provision of housing.

Housing management began under the charismatic influence of one woman. Octavia Hill felt strongly about the role of 'individuals' and tended to operate through a network of followers who in turn worked through large numbers of women volunteers. After her death, however, housing management developed into a paid profession, and Octavia Hill trained workers formed themselves in 1916 into the Association of Women House Property Managers which later became the Society of Women Housing Managers. The Society made a distinctive contribution to the development of housing management. They emphasized that management, as opposed simply to house building, was an important element in the solution to housing problems, and that housing management was an integrated function involving rent collection, dealing with repairs, and 'welfare' work. These principles can be seen as feminine although not necessarily feminist, because of their emphasis on the personal relationship between the woman housing manager and the woman tenant, and on the importance of the personal qualities of the worker, as opposed simply to her technical qualifications.

During the inter-war years women housing managers were employed in growing numbers, initially by housing associations, but increasingly by local authorities. A broad consensus of opinion agreed that this was 'women's work' because it touched on the home. Lord Astor argued that: 'The qualifications for women in housing work are at present a natural development of their closer association with the home and its shell.' (*Manchester and Salford Woman Citizen* 15 July 1927, p. 9.)

The Central Housing Advisory Committee (CHAC), a government sponsored body set up in 1935 to advise on housing matters, conducted a wide ranging review of housing management and concluded that the welfare side of housing management required the employment of women (CHAC, 1938). At the same time, women's organizations interested in enlarging the sphere of women's work repeatedly called for more women housing managers to be employed. (e.g. Ministry of Reconstruction, 1918; National Council of Women *Annual Council,* 1929.)

This apparent consensus masked, however, a growing split between the SWHM and the male dominated Institute of Housing. The latter represented anyone working in the broad area of housing – for example those involved in housing finance in local authority Treasurers Departments – rather than housing management workers. Whilst the IH endorsed the need for women workers, they argued that 'welfare' should be a specialized function separated from technical and business tasks which would be the responsibility of a housing manager with predominantly technical qualifications such as surveying. In effect 'women's work' would become ancillary to male professions in a functionally divided rather than generic service. (See minutes of the Central Housing Advisory Committee in Public Records Office location HLG 36/14.)

By the mid-1930s the IH was the larger of the two organizations, but the SWHM had a more coherent identity and was restricted to trained women only. A more restricted and highly qualified membership did not, however, place them in a stronger position to control entry to the profession and thus secure their own position: whilst membership of the SWHM remained static, the IH grew, until in 1965 the two organizations agreed to amalgamate. In the period 1965 to 1977, the percentage of qualified women and the number of women in senior housing posts fell (Brion and Tinker, 1980).

What lessons can be drawn from this history? In the first place, women's adoption of housing management as a profession for women was firmly located in a romantic framework. This both strengthened and weakened women's position. It strengthened it because it gave women a moral and intellectual rationale and sense of identity in their struggle for a sphere of women's work. It mobilized broader support from organizations such as the National Council of Women and the Women's Citizens Associations who shared this outlook. Once the SWHM agreed to admit men, as they did in 1948, their impetus seems to have been eroded (Brion and Tinker, 1980).

On the other hand, women's struggle in the occupational hierarchy was to some extent weakened by their adoption of a particular model of 'women's work'. In particular, their stress on the personal relationship between housing manager and tenant led to an emphasis on practical common sense as the main qualification needed. The SWHM argued that 'personality (sympathetic but not sentimental)' and practical abilities were the basis of the work. This personalized approach served dominant interests in so far as it provided for a more effective form of social control. Thus, it could be argued:

> It must be evident that any trained woman with tact, sympathy and understanding who visits homes weekly, easily gains the confidence of the tenant and so is in a unique position to befriend the family. Without appearing inquisitive and interfering she is able to gain all sorts of information that is more reliable than any obtained by an outsider investigating for a special purpose. ... She very easily finds out whether nonpayment of rent is due to real hardship or merely to laxity. (Reiss, 1935, p. 7.)

On the other hand, such a personalized approach was not necessarily favoured by the men who held a dominant position in local authorities as councillors or existing housing workers. The discussions amongst the members of the Central Housing Advisory Committee provide an interesting insight into their thinking. Some thought that 'social service' in the Housing Department was costly and wasteful; others thought that it involved too great an intervention into the home – it was 'life management' rather than housing management argued Mr Ling from Derby. Finally the male technical professionals, architects and surveyors, had already carved out a dominant position in housing departments and were not planning to relinquish it (see public records office H.L.G. 37/14). The rivalry between the IH and the SWHM was thus a struggle between men and women with conflicting professional interests and ideas about the nature of the service to be provided.

(ii) Social work

Social work as a paid career for women owes its emergence to two developments: the movement to regulate the giving of charity through careful review of each case, and the development of statutory social services. The former was particularly associated with the Charity Organisation Society (COS) founded in 1869 to regulate alms giving such that only the deserving were helped, and in such a way as to be consistent with maintaining the recipient's independence and self-respect. From this movement developed the idea of social casework and, from the turn of the century the beginnings of social work training (Woodroofe, 1962).

Unlike housing management, however, the leading pioneers of social work tended to be men. Thus, despite the fact that most of the visitors who assessed the means and morals of the poor were women, the leading figures who controlled the COS were predominantly men – Octavia Hill was indeed the only woman on the first council. Nevertheless, men were happy to inaugurate areas of work for women where they could in effect be the helpmates of men. Thus Charles Loch, a leading figure in the COS, is credited with the idea of hospital social work (almoning), but this developed from 1895 onwards as an exclusively female profession (Walton, 1975).

Social work during the inter-war years saw a steady albeit slow growth, but it remained linked primarily to voluntary bodies. Only probation officers achieved statutory recognition when their attachment to courts was made compulsory in 1925. At the time, this formed the only area of social work which was dominated by men (Walton, 1975). In general, social work was a female occupation that was poorly paid and relied heavily on single women.

In the years after the Second World War, the expansion of statutory social services increased the demand for social workers as part of local authority services. Post-war concern about child neglect led to the statutory requirement in the 1948 Children Act that local authorities set up Children's Departments, and there was an increase in concern over the training and status of social workers. These developments have led to an increase in hierarchy within social work and the emergence of managerial posts within local authorities offering better salaries and career prospects. These developments have been associated with the same process of masculine colonization in the profession that we saw in the case of housing management, although there was no equivalent direct struggle between the sexes. Thus Walton argues that as early as the 1950s, men were taking double the number of managerial posts in comparison to their percentage in the profession. Since 1970 the process has been accelerated by the reorganization of local authority personal social services. The overwhelming majority of heads of the 160 new Social Services Departments were men and, perhaps more alarming, the number of women has continued to decline from sixteen in 1971 to twelve in 1984. A recent report argues that, despite the fact that 60 per cent of workers in Social Services Departments are women, they have no better chance of reaching top jobs in Social Services than in the more traditionally male technical departments (Local Government Operational Research Unit, 1984).

Once again, women seem to have been caught in a double bind: the romantic view of women's role enabled social work to develop as a woman's profession – but with concomitant low salaries and prestige. However: 'Once the special arguments for regarding certain areas of work as women's work disappeared it seemed inevitable that eventually men would step in to the major controlling positions.' (Walton, 1975, p. 235.)

(iii) Health visiting

The third area of women's work which developed out of philanthropy was health visiting. Unlike social work, health visiting had its origins in preventive health rather than charity: in particular, in the work of the Manchester and Salford Ladies Sanitary Reform Association founded in 1860. Like other philanthropists, the Manchester Ladies emphasized immediate action on the problem rather than wider ideas of social reform, and saw themselves as a kind of health missionary bearing the religion of hygiene not the Bible: 'The disinfectant powder and the medical soap are the keys by which the hearts and doors are opened.' (1872 *Annual Report* quoted in Gates, 1938, p. 11.)

Whether the poor welcomed being disinfected in this way is a moot point. Nevertheless, the emphasis on preventive health meant that the health missionaries were not obsessed with separating the deserving and undeserving as was the COS, neither did they have the COS's power to withhold financial help.

Health visiting gradually gained statutory backing – initially at local level when Manchester City Council brought the Ladies' Association under the umbrella of its Medical Officer of Health, and later nationally after the 1904 Committee on Physical Deterioration recommended a nationally co-ordinated health visiting service. The development of a national service gained further impetus in 1907 when notification of births became compulsory. At the same time, the status of the profession was raised by new training requirements, and in 1908 the Royal Sanitary Institute began to set examinations and award qualifications.

We have already referred to some differences between health visiting and the COS. Dingwall (1977) goes further, and argues that health visiting is essentially collectivist in inspiration and, up until the First World War, was distinctively radical in outlook, with many health visitors coming from working class backgrounds. This radicalism he sees as being dissipated after the First World War as part of a move to professionalism and a defeat of feminism.

The picture drawn by Dingwall is at odds with what we would expect from the history of housing management and social work. Whilst philanthropy had humanitarian aspects, it could hardly be called radical or collectivist, and feminists generally fought for women to gain a foothold in the world of professionals rather than opposing professionalism. Recent research by Carolyn Taylor in Manchester casts doubt on the validity of Dingwall's account. Early health visiting was riven with class distinctions, with the 'lady volunteers' of the sanitary societies employing working-class women as health visitors. When the local authorities became more involved, they were dissatisfied with both the 'ladies' and the working-class health visitors, favouring middle-class women with nursing qualifications. This displacement of working class women began long before the First World War, a fact confirmed in passing by Jean Donnison in her study of the registration of midwives. Under the 1902 Midwives Act, supervision was often carried out by health visitors: 'Women generally of higher social status than midwives, but with little or no practical experience of midwifery, who in consequence were resented by midwives as ignorant and overbearing.' (Donnison, 1977, p. 182.)

Similarly, Carolyn Taylor argues that 'collectivism' amounted to little more than knocking on a lot of doors! The primary role of health visitors was the education of mothers: a role which placed them firmly in the individualist mould of social intervention.

It would appear that the development of health visiting led to feminists facing the same contradictions and ambiguities. Yes, greater opportunities were opening up for women as welfare workers, who also brought with them a genuine concern for their women clients. However, in the process, class hierarchies amongst women were reproduced in the Welfare State, and middle-class women became involved in judging working-class mothers.

5 Conclusion

What impact did women's entry into welfare professions have on the Welfare State, and in particular, did they make welfare services more responsive to the needs of the women who used them? The picture we have drawn is a mixed one. We referred earlier to the ideas of Ehrenreich and English who suggest that women face two possible models on which to base their entry into the public sphere: the romantic and the rationalist. To a considerable extent, women entered medicine on the rationalist model. Whilst they benefited women patients by giving them the choice of consulting a woman doctor if they wished to, they did not voice the kinds of criticism of modern technological medicine or the medicalization of childbirth which concern many contemporary feminists. This should not, however, be taken as a major criticism of the first women doctors. As we saw in chapter 1, feminist campaigners in the inter-war years wanted more hospital births, and perhaps only the experience of universal health provision has given us the luxury of questioning whether it really does us any good!

The women pioneers of new areas of welfare work seemed, by way of contrast, to have largely accommodated themselves to the romantic view that women have special qualities. This should not be regarded in a wholly negative light. The women often stressed issues such as the importance of personal qualities and personal relationships as opposed to the male tendency to see the professional role in a more impersonal and technocratic way. Women today sometimes argue that women welfare providers can respond better to women's needs than male professionals, and have a more open and less hierarchical approach to the worker–client relationship. They too are therefore arguing that women have special qualities. On the other hand, the emphasis on women's role *vis-à-vis* the home is not an argument about women's qualities, but about their *role*. This meant that women's movement out of the home into the public sphere was achieved without any fundamental challenge to the dominant ideology that women's role is in the home. It is this ideology that contemporary feminists challenge because they believe that it underpins women's oppression.

Our assessment of the role of the women pioneers must also highlight the social class divisions between women which they reinforced. The new professions were made up of middle-class women who were very much involved in the social control of working class mothers. Although individual women such as Margaret Llewellyn Davies, a sanitary inspector and leading member of the Women's Co-operative Guild, used her knowledge of working-class poverty to campaign for extensions to the Welfare State, the majority of the new professionals did not. Instead, they emphasized individual casework, and can be seen as middle class women attempting to inculcate middle-class values into working-class homes.

The role of women professionals as agents of social control has led Donzelot (1980) and others to see the movement for the extension of women's rights as inextricably bound up with the development of new forms of social discipline whereby state control becomes very much part of daily life. Donzelot describes this as the 'patriarchy of the state' which effectively displaced the older form of family patriarchy whereby male heads of households controlled other family members. Donzelot argues that women in alliance with the new professionals and technocrats acted as the agents of this new discipline. Women's position in society was advanced as a result, and thus feminism and the new patriarchy became entrenched at the expense of the working class (Donzelot, 1980).

Donzelot's analysis has been criticized by Barrett and McIntosh (1982) for a barely veiled anti-feminism and nostalgia for the older form of patriarchy. We share their view that too much emphasis is being placed on women's role as the human link in the chain of social control. Equally, if not more important, were the impersonal forms of social control embodied in national insurance and other forms of social legislation. Nevertheless, we cannot avoid the conclusions that the development of women's professions advanced the interests of middle class women to some extent at the expense of working-class women, and that the role of women in judging other women remains an important, but neglected area of feminist criticism of the Welfare State today (see David, 1985).

Part II:

Contemporary feminism and the critique of welfare

3

Contemporary feminism

1 Introduction

In the rest of the book, we shall be looking at the ideas and activities of feminists today. Many of the issues confronting contemporary feminists are little different from those which faced our sisters who took part in the first wave of feminist activity. Women may have won the vote, but politics is still largely a man's world. Post-war economic growth and the extension of the Welfare State have improved women's material position, but many still experience poverty, and their standard of living tends to be lower on average than men's. The extension of state secondary and higher education has increased the number of well qualified women, but equality of opportunity for women has not been achieved.

Where many of today's feminists part company, however, with the earlier generation, is in their attitude to women's position in the home. Whilst there have always been feminists who have argued in favour of economic independence for all women, mainstream feminism as it developed in the first half of this century tended to extol family life, and accepted the sexual division of labour in the home which designated the male as breadwinner, and his wife as economically dependent on him, and responsible for child care and housework. Despite different views within feminism as to how radical the changes need to be in the family, all feminists now see women as disadvantaged by the pressure – both material and ideological – to perform a role which leaves them doing isolated, low status unpaid work within the home.

Similarly, whilst early twentieth century and contemporary feminists share a critique of the double standard of sexual morality, and have exposed the way men have manipulated women's sexuality in order to obtain both domestic and sexual services, most earlier feminists saw the solution as persuading men to live up to the standards set for women. Today, feminists are far more likely to be concerned with sexual freedom – 'the right to a self-defined sexuality' – which would allow women to choose freely between lesbianism, heterosexual 'free love', monogamy or celibacy. Whilst some feminists come close to the attitudes of earlier feminists in rejecting permissiveness as simply a new form of male exploitation of women's sexuality, their starting point is very different.

We shall now explore these three areas of concern – women's role in public life, the home, and sexuality – from the perspective of contemporary feminism.

2 Women in the public sphere: continued inequality

Despite having won equal political rights with men, the removal of legal barriers to entry to professions, and the extension of secondary and higher education, women are still dramatically underrepresented in positions of political and economic power in society.

Women have been allowed to stand for Parliament since 1918, and finally achieved an equal franchise in 1928. Since then they have made relatively little progress in gaining greater political representation. In the 1979 General Election only 8 per cent of the candidates were women, yet this was the highest percentage ever. Women have never formed more than 4.5 per cent of MPs. These figures reflect a number of factors: women do not put themselves forward for selection as often as men; they are selected for fewer safe seats; and they are more likely to stand for smaller parties where they have less chance of being elected. However, the percentage of women candidates for minority parties tends to decline as they begin to gain electoral success. At local government level women are better represented, but still form no more than a substantial minority at under 20 per cent of councillors (Stacey and Price, 1981; Wormald, 1982).

Turning to economic power, women's position is little better. Women's participation in the labour force has been growing steadily this century. In 1911, only 10 per cent of married women worked, whilst by 1980 the figure had increased sixfold to 62 per cent. Nevertheless, women tend to remain ghettoized in low paid, unskilled, 'women's jobs'. The typical woman worker is either an unskilled manual worker in one of the newer, light industries or public services, or a white collar worker involved in clerical or secretarial work in the service sector. Many of the occupations in which they are found are almost exclusively the preserve of women: more than 90 per cent of typists, secretaries and canteen assistants, for example, are women. Many women are classed as 'low paid', and despite a narrowing of the gap between male and female earnings during the early and mid-1970s, women's earnings seem now to have become fixed on the ratchet of around three quarters of men's.

Very few women are found in professional or managerial posts. In 1919, the legal profession was opened to women, but in January 1983, only 11.9 per cent of members of the Law Society were women, whilst the Institute of Chartered Accountants has 5.8 per cent women members. Women form a mere 2 per cent of the British Institute of Management. (Figures supplied by the EOC.) Only in welfare professions do women seem to have made any headway.

Women's position in the labour market is reflected in their absence from positions of power in the corporate bodies which represent the major economic interest groups in society. Not surprisingly, given their absence from managerial positions, women are almost invisible in the CBI. Women are not, however, absent from the trade union movement: they make up around a third of trade union membership, and form the majority in some unions. (NUPE, the public services manual workers union, has 67 per cent women members, for example.) This is not, however, reflected in numbers of women paid officials, or representation at the level of their National Executives.

The early feminists were mainly concerned with removing formal barriers which barred women from entering certain professions. More recently, feminists have pressed for public policies to outlaw discrimination against women – direct discrimination such as paying a woman less than a man doing the same job, or indirect discrimination, such as attaching unnecessary conditions to a job which will have the effect of excluding women. Such anti-discrimination legislation is represented by the 1970 Equal Pay Act and the 1975 Sex Discrimination Act. The figures on women's labour market position which we quoted earlier indicate that such legislation has had little impact on women's economic position. Increasingly, feminists of all persuasions are coming to agree that women's position in the public spheres of work and politics cannot be viewed in isolation from their role in the private sphere of home and family. Feminists today argue that 'the personal is political' because we cannot understand women's unequal position in society unless we look at so-called personal issues: in particular the way in which the feminine gender role comes to be constructed and maintained, and the way in which the sexual division of labour in the home conditions women's lives in both the public and private sphere.

3 'The problem that has no name'

In 1965 Betty Friedan's book *The Feminine Mystique* was published, the first of a number of feminist writings to argue that the prevailing cultural norm required women to subordinate their active and creative needs in order to conform to the feminine image and housewife role. As a result, stay-at-home women felt empty and dissatisfied, tired and depressed. Friedan argued that:

> The problem that has no name – which is simply the fact that American women are kept from growing to their full human capacities – is taking a far greater toll on the physical and mental health of our country than any known disease.
> (Friedan, 1965, p. 318.)

Friedan's book is in the best traditions of feminist writing in that it grows directly out of women's experience. It is, however, essentially the experience of white, middle class suburban America. The 'feminine mystique' did not affect all women in the same way – many working-class women, especially black working-class women, still had to do the double shift of low paid jobs and unpaid housework, in poor, overcrowded homes.

Nevertheless, social changes in Britain since the Second World War have in many respects narrowed the gap between the experience of middle and working class women. Middle-class women have become 'proletarianized' due to the disappearance of domestic servants, whilst the burden of housework on working-class women has gradually been lightened due to improvements in housing conditions, the almost universal introduction of electricity and increased availability of consumer durables.

All these changes have the potential for broadening women's

lives beyond the traditional limits of family, home and immediate neighbourhood. During the Second World War, new horizons had opened up for women when they were drawn into the labour force to replace men, and housework and childcare were partly socialized through the establishment of communal eating facilities – the 'British Restaurants' – and more extensive nursery provision. Although this nursery provision was never adequate to meet the demand for places from women workers, after the war the nurseries and restaurants were closed and women were encouraged to stay at home. This process was reinforced by a new ideology which stressed that young children needed full-time mothers (see Riley, 1983a).

Alongside the state and the experts, commercial interests also promoted the image of women as housewives and mothers who, in this case were central to the process of consumption. The privatized, home centred life-style premised on the stay-at-home wife provided an ideal market for the new mass-produced consumer goods which flooded into the shops during the 'affluent' 1950s and 1960s.

Until Friedan and her sisters sparked off the second wave of the women's liberation movement, organized women by and large went along with this dominant ideology. Organization such as the Council for Scientific Management in the Home (CSMH) stressed the need for housework's drudgery to be minimized not so that women could be liberated, but in the interests of national and industrial efficiency. In a CSMH pamphlet with the engaging title of 'Housework with Satisfaction', Mildred Wheatcroft argues:

> The more productive the home and the smaller the strain of domestic work on the housewife, the better will be the health of the future generation, the smaller the national resources devoted to health and other welfare services, the more efficient and happy the workers in industry. (Wheatcroft (ed.), 1960, p. 16.)

And what will *women* get out of it? The question is not even posed – although elsewhere in the same publication, the problem of boredom in the kitchen is seen as being mitigated by the placing of sinks and cookers near windows rather than blank walls!

In Britain, the explosion of feminist writing and activity did not begin until the 1970s. Nevertheless, in their isolated homes, many British women were experiencing the same dissatisfaction which Friedan described for American women. In 1966 Hannah

Gavron published *The Captive Wife* based on her Phd study of
the experience of women with young children. The majority of
the women she interviewed had worked before having children,
and had given up paid work on the birth of their first child. Their
feelings of boredom, isolation and lack of purpose in their lives
are remarkably close to those of American women:

> 'Being at home all day is terribly boring, frustrating and to my
> mind very *inferior*', was one comment. Another said, 'Bored?
> I'm just fed up', and another, 'I am haunted by a sense of
> wasted time' ... In fact *all* mothers in this sample who had
> worked after they were married said they were often bored at
> home and a quarter complained of being lonely as well.
> (Gavron, 1966, p. 111.)

Several years after Gavron's work, and after the turmoil of the
late 1960s, we find Anne Oakley portraying a picture of ordinary
women's lives as largely unchanged. Oakley interviewed forty
housewives, again from a broad spectrum of social classes.
Although attitudes to housework varied according to factors such
as education, all housewives were dissatisfied with their role: both
because of its low status and lack of reward, and the inherent
monotony and fragmentation in the tasks having to be
performed. This dissatisfaction was not always clearly articulated
as such: women could be resistant to the idea of denigrating their
role as if it were tantamount to denigrating themselves (Oakley,
1974).

There is a deeper point at issue here: many women argue that
the women's movement has failed to offer realistic and satisfying
alternatives to traditional roles for the majority of women. In
chapter 7 we shall be considering the arguments of some women
that it would be preferable to attempt to raise the status and
rewards of motherhood rather than encouraging more women to
work outside the home. Regardless of the position one takes in
this debate, however, all feminists agree that women should have
genuine *choices* as to their role in society. These are denied in
present day society both by the ideology that women should be
full-time mothers, and the low status and rewards of the role.

4 Out of the closet – women and sexuality

Sexuality is an issue which causes major divisions between women
when it comes to discussing *strategy*. Nevertheless, almost all

feminists agree that manipulation of women's sexuality occurs, and that women should have the right to choice and self-definition in this area as much as any other.

Feminists argue that women's sexuality is controlled by men or male dominated institutions in four ways. First, commercial interests use women's bodies to sell everything from toilet cleaners to sports cars. The image of women presented in advertising is either of the asexual housewife, or the sexually seductive temptress. In both cases she is defined in terms of *others*: as the housewife, she has no sexuality, her role being to care for the home and mother her husband and children; as the sultry sex-object she is designed to arouse erotic feelings in the male customer.

Women have also been manipulated by experts and professionals who have elevated male-orientated psychological and social theories into universal truths, or male prejudice into professional judgment. We shall be exploring this issue in greater detail in the next two chapters, since welfare professionals have played a key role in this area.

It would be hard to find any contemporary feminists who disagreed with the above two paragraphs. Controversy becomes more evident, however, when we look at the other mechanisms which feminists see as limiting women's sexual freedom of choice: the institution of marriage and the family, and male violence against women.

'The family' is a term that can mean any number of things: hippy communes have called themselves 'families'; single people whose kin live on the opposite side of the world have 'families'; the Conservative Cabinet's 1983 Family Policy Group's deliberations were mainly about the role of professionals and the state in welfare provision. The *dominant* meaning of family is of a heterosexual married couple with children. This is the *form* of the family. The values associated with this form include privacy, fulfilment within the bounds of family relationships, and socialization of children towards individual achievement. We shall refer to this as the 'bourgeois family', not in any spirit of rancour, but because it is an appropriate name for the family form and way of life which became dominant amongst bourgeois families of the Victorian period, and gradually spread throughout other social classes.

The bourgeois family is dominant as an ideal in our society since those who choose alternative living arrangements and values are seen as deviating from this ideal norm – by remaining single, remaining childless, living as a lesbian couple or as single parent families – and as a consequence suffer social penalties. These penalties operate in a number of ways. First, everyone is expected to be part of a family, for the sake of their own health and happiness. The modern family is seen as a haven in an alienated world, and those who remain single are often viewed with pity. This has always oppressed women more than men, since the sexual double standard and the greater weight given to woman's sexuality in her overall fulfilment have created the 'spinster' as a frustrated, miserable creature compared with the bachelor!

Pity moves to disapproval when women transgress the norms of motherhood associated with the bourgeois family. Too many children, particularly if the mother is not financially secure, indicates fecklessness, but women who choose not to have children, particularly married women, frequently have to face incomprehension and even overt hostility from their doctors, other welfare experts, and indeed from their own friends and relatives. According to Jean Veevers:

> Persons (and particularly women) who opt for a childfree marriage are continually being asked to explain why they do not want children. Friends and relatives feel that they have a right to know; doctors and amateur psychiatrists hope to be able to help with the 'problem' (Veevers, 1980, p. 136).

Finally, disapproval may move to social ostracism when women reject heterosexual marriage altogether and choose lesbianism. This particularly affects lesbian mothers, who live in fear of having their children taken away from them.

When women speak of 'violence against women' they may refer to a range of ways in which men control women. The most obvious manifestation is men's violence against the women with whom they live. There have been many attempts to explain such violence, many of which involve 'blaming the victim' – for example Gayford's concept of the provocative woman or Erin Pizzey's theory of an 'addiction to violence' on the part of some women (Pizzey and Shapiro, 1982). In contrast, feminists argue that male violence is the ultimate sanction employed by men to retain their authority in the home:

> Far from being abnormal behaviour, the violence of men towards the women they live with should rather be seen as an extreme form of normality, an exaggeration of how society expects men to behave – as the authority figure in the family. The search for causation then becomes a wild goose chase,

because it is concerned with wider issues to do with the control
of women by men, to do with power and inequality, and to do
with how we perceive manhood. (Wilson, 1983, p. 95.)

More controversially, some feminists argue that pornography
violates women and thus *is violence*, and support campaigns
against the circulation of such material. Others are anxious lest
feminism become a new social purity movement. Most would,
however, agree with Elizabeth Wilson that 'some pornography is
still so deeply offensive, so violent and so degrading to women
that its free circulation is something we should protest against'.
(Wilson, 1983, p. 154.)

We have returned to where we began in this section on
sexuality: women do not want to have their sexuality defined in
male terms, whether as soothing mother figures selling cough
cures, as tame, sexy 'bits-of-fluff' selling tabloid newspapers, or as
the objects of wilder sado-masochistic fantasy!

5 The Women's Movement today

In our review of the views of contemporary feminists on the
nature of women's oppression we have inevitably touched on
some of the issues which divide the women's movement today. In
the remainder of this chapter we will explore these divisions in
greater depth and attempt to categorize the different strands of
feminism in terms of their goals for women and their assumptions
and theories about the nature and causes of oppression. We shall
look at three groups of feminists, all of whom have been active
around welfare issues: liberal feminists, radical feminists and
socialist feminists. Despite the difficulty and danger of forcing
the varied strands of feminism into water-tight categories, some
such categorization is necessary if we are to be able to make sense
of the varied and contradictory goals of women in the
movement.

(i) Liberal feminism

The most obvious continuity between contemporary and early
twentieth century feminism is in the liberal tradition, with its
demand for equal rights and the removal of legal and political
discrimination against women. Whilst many of the older liberal

feminist organizations such as the Six Point Group and the Women's Freedom League folded during the 1960s, the present upsurge has given liberal feminism a new impetus.

Liberal feminism is about equal rights and equal opportunities. The four main planks of liberal feminism involve the removal of discrimination against women; the attempt to place more women in positions of power, through increasing their representation in politics and on public bodies; encouraging and enabling more women to gain higher paid, prestigious jobs; and the attempt to provide equal opportunities for girls by combating sex discrimination and sex stereotyping in schools. An organization like the Equal Opportunities Commission (EOC) may be regarded as a good example of this current. The EOC was set up under the 1975 Sex Discrimination Act, and is primarily concerned with the elimination of formal sex discrimination. It acts on behalf of individual women – and indeed men – who believe they have been unjustly treated on the grounds of their sex. It has also sponsored research, and promoted projects such as Women Into Science and Engineering which encourages girls to take science subjects in schools, and consider engineering as a possible career.

The EOC has not limited itself entirely to equal rights issues, however. It has produced reports on issues such as minimum wages policies, and the problems facing women who care for adult dependants, which are more accurately described as 'reformist' – piecemeal reforms to improve women's material position. It is, indeed, difficult always to isolate a specific liberal feminist current in the women's movement. Many feminists who see themselves as socialist or radical may support liberal or reformist proposals as part of a wider programme of more radical change, rather than as ends in themselves. The difference between these feminists and the EOC may be as much to do with *how* they campaign for change as the actual demands raised. Whilst socialist feminists may seek to link such issues to a wider anti-capitalist struggle, liberal-reformists tend to rely on a pressure group approach to policy makers – an approach which presupposes a relatively open, pluralist policy making process. Like the EOC, Rights of Women (ROW), an 'organisation of women legal workers', is primarily concerned with problems of legal discrimination against women. It would be misleading, however, to characterize ROW as 'liberal feminist', since most of the women involved would see women's liberation as involving more fundamental change than legal reform. Furthermore in raising issues such as discrimination against lesbian mothers (ROW 1984), ROW steps across that invisible line which divides the more reformist-consensual politics of the EOC from the women's liberation movement.

In conclusion we would argue that, whilst we can can see the hallmarks of liberal feminism in many proposals for reform of welfare today, particularly in relation to education, we need to be cautious in labelling all equal rights approaches in this way. In Part III, when we come to look at feminist campaigns today, we shall often use the category liberal-reformist to refer to those who favour working co-operatively with men to remove discrimination or introduce piecemeal reforms, without questioning whether the institutions themselves need to be changed more fundamentally to eliminate sex and class bias, or whether there is any conflict of interest between men and women. It is socialist and radical feminists who have spearheaded, both in theory and practice, this more radical challenge to sexism in society.

(ii) Radical feminism

Radical feminism lies at the opposite end of the spectrum to liberal feminism, and has little in common with the earlier generation of feminists. Far from seeking co-operation with men, radical feminists believe that men and women belong to antagonistic classes. From time immemorial men have dominated and controlled women, physically and mentally, in a social system described as 'patriarchal'. The term patriarchy literally means 'rule by the father' and whilst radical feminists today do not necessarily see male power as rooted in the power of fathers as such they use the term to denote men's power as a *class* over women. Many radical feminists argue that sexual oppression is the root from which all other oppressions flow – the question is not then how patriarchal social relations interact with capitalism or racism, but how patriarchy creates the conditions in which other forms of oppression can arise (Firestone, 1979).

This definition of patriarchy as the root of all oppression shifts the focus of attention of many radical feminists to the biological differences between men and women. Patriarchy is the system whereby men control women. It predates all other forms of domination, and has *always* existed: hence it is explained by reference to timeless biological factors. Firestone argues that women's social and economic disadvantage stems from their role in biological reproduction, and that women's liberation depends on *society* taking responsibility for biological reproduction, through the development of the foetus outside women's bodies.

This idea has been taken up by the novelist Marge Piercy, whose vision of a utopian future in *Woman on the Edge of Time* includes small groups of men and women collectively rearing children born, not of women, but in a kind of baby production unit of artificial wombs.

This biologically determinist strand of radical feminism offers little perspective on how to develop action now, and many women are suspicious of an approach which relies on developments in reproductive technology – an area of research currently controlled by men.

Many radical feminists have stressed instead the way biological differences in physical strength and aggression have enabled men to control women through the threat of physical violence. Radical feminists do not argue that all men *are* violent, but they suggest that all men are complicit in keeping women in a state of fear. Susan Brownmiller applies this argument to her study of rape, which she sees as: 'nothing more or less than a conscious process of intimidation by which *all* men keep *all* women in a state of fear.' (Brownmiller, 1976, p. 26. Emphasis in original.)

Radical feminist theory does not lead in the direction of seeking equality with men, but towards rejection of men, their values and the institutions they have created. It could, indeed, be said to point in the direction of 'matriarchy'.

How have these approaches affected the campaigns of radical feminists? Since women in different economic positions tend to express different interests, the distinctive contribution of radical feminism has been in areas where women are clearly oppressed as a sex: in particular in their critique of male violence, and their demand for the right to a self-defined sexuality which is denied by the pressures which impel women into monogamous, heterosexual marriage and prevent lesbianism being seen as a valid alternative. Radical feminists have placed special emphasis on campaigns which highlight the issue of male violence against women, in particular around the issues of rape, pornography and battered women. From the mid-1970s, radical feminism has provided the impetus which has led to women's 'Reclaim the Night' marches, pickets of sex shops and other such campaigns. Many feminists who do not regard themselves as radical feminists of course supported these campaigns, and Women's Aid refuges for battered women or Rape Crisis Centres also provide a meeting ground for radical and socialist feminists. Nevertheless, it is probably true that without the radical feminist impetus, these campaigns might not have got off the ground in the first place.

The second distinctive contribution of radical feminism is the idea of separatism. Within radical feminism there is a spectrum of views on this issue from those who argue for *political* separatism, to those who argue for total political and *personal* separatism from men. Amongst the latter are those who advocate 'political lesbianism' – the refusal to engage in sexual relationships with men. Heterosexual relationships are seen as consorting with the enemy:

> In it each individual woman comes under the control of an individual man ... In the couple, love and sex are used to obscure the realities of oppression, to prevent women identifying with each other in order to revolt, and from identifying 'their' man as part of the enemy. Any woman who takes part in a heterosexual couple helps to shore up male supremacy. (Leeds Revolutionary Feminist Group, 1982, p. 64.)

Radical feminists have also been prominent in the women's peace movement, because they see peace and our survival as a species as peculiarly women's issues. Women's values are seen as supportive of peace, whilst men are seen as aggressors whose competitive values and resort to inter-personal violence underlie militarism and warfare.

This particular strand within feminism has brought the WLM into a seemingly contradictory position. Feminism emerged in opposition to the anti-feminists' view that women's subordinate position was all part of the natural order, yet here we find feminists arguing that biological differences do matter, that women have 'special qualities' and that these are connected to values of caring and non-violence. Liberal feminists have not been slow to challenge this viewpoint, since it appears to undermine the equal rights case which is based fairly and squarely on the argument that the categories male and female should be irrelevant when deciding on social arrangements:

> regarding peace and such things as women's values, or women's concern, is in effect to accept the idea of the separate spheres, as well as to perpetuate the myth that the problem about the position of men and women has to do with what their values are. (Richards, 1983, p. 8.)

Not all radical feminists share this emphasis on biology in their understanding of women's oppression. In particular, the French feminist Christine Delphy has developed a theoretical approach which she refers to as 'materialist radical feminism'. This approach shares with Marxism the idea that people's values and interests are shaped primarily by the social relationships arising from the way in which any society organizes itself to produce the basic necessities of life. Like Marxists, she refers to different ways of organizing production as different 'modes of production'.

From here onwards Delphy parts company with socialist/ Marxist feminists who argue that in present day capitalist societies the mode of *production* is capitalist where as patriarchal social relationships have their base in the family which is the site of *reproduction*. Delphy, however, argues that the family is equally a mode of production, a 'patriarchal mode of production' which produces goods and services for consumption in the same way as the capitalist enterprise. Marriage is thus seen as a 'labour contract' in which the wife is the employee providing services – the cook, dish washer, cleaner – whilst her husband is the beneficiary of these services, in return for which he 'pays' her by providing full or partial upkeep. The man and woman in marriage are thus seen as members of opposing classes. Although Delphy acknowledges that capitalism also creates opposed classes, she argues that, for women, men are 'the main enemy'. (Delphy, 1984.)

(iii) Socialist feminism

Turning to socialist feminism, we also find that the link with the feminists we described in chapter 1 is weak. The working class women whom we looked at owed their allegiance to the labour movement organizations from which they sprang – for example, the Women's Co-operative Guild saw itself as part of a broad co-operative movement rather than a women's movement, and was oriented towards practical reforms to improve women's lives. Contemporary socialist feminism has its roots in the Marxist-oriented left groups rather than the broad labour movement. Many contemporary feminists were active in the upsurge of radical politics of the late 1960s where they discovered that socialist rhetoric could combine all too easily with sexist practices (for an amusing account of life in the Young Socialists, see Rowbotham, 1973a) and have seen their role as having two aspects: promoting women's interests through the women's movement, and attempting to bring a better awareness of gender and personal issues into the socialist movement.

Socialist feminists have played a crucial role in the reformulation of orthodox Marxist theory which is sadly lacking in two ways: it is gender-blind, refusing to examine the specific position of women, and it has virtually no analysis of the family. Socialist feminists' starting point is that the capitalist mode of production cannot be analysed simply in terms of capital and labour – the relationship between those who own/control the means of production, and those who work for them in return for a wage. Capitalist *production*, the central concern of Marxism, relies for its continued operation on a system of social and biological *reproduction* which takes place in the home, an area which has received virtually no attention from orthodox Marxism.

Early socialist feminist critiques of Marxist theory attempted to explain the relationship between capitalism and the family in strictly economic terms. Women's unpaid labour in the home was seen as directly or indirectly increasing the profits of capitalists, who were able to pay their (male) workers less than the true costs of their daily upkeep as fit, healthy workers. Women working for nothing in the home could thus be seen as working for capitalists in the home rather than the factory.

This 'domestic labour debate' sparked off a series of articles, and the precise relationship between housework and profit seemed an important issue at the time (several of these articles are collected in Malos, 1980). In retrospect, the debate seems rather sterile. It is impossible to establish a *direct* link between the level of housework and the rate of profit, and there can be no 'iron law' that without the traditional sexual division of labour in the home, capitalists would always make lower profits – witness the position of black mine workers, *denied* their families, in South Africa.

More recent socialist feminist analysis has moved away from this economistic approach. Instead of assuming that men and women perform different economic and social roles because such an arrangement benefits capitalism, they have attempted to analyse more precisely the different mechanisms which act to reproduce the sexual division of labour and who benefits from it. They have shown that, historically, male trade unionists acted to exclude women from many occupations in order to prevent men and women competing in the labour market. They have demonstrated how women's dependent economic status gives men control over the allocation of money within the home, and that this often results in women not receiving the full benefits of increases in men's wages. (Pahl, 1980 provides interesting research evidence on the relationship between women's economic role and patterns of money management in the home.) In confronting these sorts of issues, many socialist feminists were led to argue that women's position in the home benefited men as well as capitalism.

They argued that the capitalist system might shape the particular *form* of women's oppression, but that oppression could not be *reduced* to the capitalist mode of production. This required a new theoretical basis for analysing the relations between the sexes. Many socialist feminists have therefore turned to the concept of patriarchy to provide a theoretical basis for understanding the way in which men as a group have gained a privileged position in society at the expense of women. They do not argue, as do radical feminists, that patriarchy is independent of capitalism, but instead see the two systems as interrelated – whilst patriarchal inequalities pre-date capitalism, the particular form they take today is shaped by the capitalist system.

Socialists are also suspicious of any theory which explains these power relationships in terms of biological differences. They have therefore sought to find a material base for male privilege in relations of production. Hartmann, for example, defines patriarchy as: 'a set of social relations between men, which have a material base, and which, though hierarchical, establish or create interdependence and solidarity among men that enable them to dominate women.' (Hartmann, 1981, p. 14.)

She goes on to argue that the material basis of patriarchy lies in men's control over women's labour power. Her understanding of the roots of patriarchy is not dissimilar from that of Christine Delphy. As a socialist, however, she believes that capitalism and patriarchy *together* shape women's position. Patriarchy is not seen as more important than capitalism, and men are not the main enemy. This dual approach, seeing capitalism and patriarchy as distinct but interlocking systems is found in the work of many other socialist feminists (for example, Eisenstein, 1981).

The use of the concept of patriarchy remains controversial amongst socialist feminists. Ehrenreich and English (1979) and Michele Barrett (1981) point out that the term has a literal meaning – rule by the father – and should only be used to refer to the pre-capitalist order in which authority over the family is vested in older males, and everyone knows their place in a stable, hierarchical order. They argue, that if we use the term patriarchy to refer to the many forms of male domination which have existed throughout history, women's oppression comes to be seen as timeless and unchanging, when in practice it has taken radically different forms.

Furthermore, many socialist feminists are reluctant to see class oppression being removed from its dominant position in socialist feminist theory. Barrett argues:

> in posing patriarchy as either completely independent of capitalism, or as the dominant system of power relations, it completely fails to provide an analysis of women's oppression in a society characterised by capitalist relations of production. (Barrett, 1981, p. 38.)

This theoretical difference has practical implications. Many socialist feminists are sensitive to the idea that the gender role system is not wholly in men's interests. Barrett, for example, points out that there are disadvantages for men in their role as breadwinners. This opens the door to a closer alliance between men and women in a common struggle against class *and* gender inequality. Similarly Rowbotham rejects the concept of patriarchy because it leads women to see oppression everywhere in relations between the sexes: 'Some aspects of male–female relationships are evidently not simply oppressive, but include varying degrees of mutual aid. The concept of "patriarchy" has no room for such subtleties, however.' (Rowbotham, 1981, p. 74.)

Socialist feminism therefore represents a spectrum of theory and practice. Those who give primacy to oppression rooted in social class have campaigned for reforms which will be of particular benefit to working-class women, and which simultaneously challenge capitalist economic and social relationships. Perhaps the classic example is the Working Women's Charter Campaign in the early 1970s which attempted to gain support from (male dominated) labour movement organizations for demands such as equal pay, maternity leave, childcare and rights to contraception and abortion. At the other end of the spectrum, socialist women have joined with their radical feminist sisters in taking up issues such as male violence against women, which focus more directly on men's oppression of women.

6 Class, race and gender

Feminism and the women's movement attempt to speak to all women and to represent their interests as a sex. In practice, however, women's interests are not always clearcut. We saw in Chapter 1 how feminists were often divided by social class. Although class divisions are less pronounced today, they still exist. The main beneficiaries of liberal feminist campaigns have been white, middle class women, and most socialist and radical feminists are middle class: they have had varying degrees of success in their attempts to speak to the needs and experiences of working class women. Today there is a further dimension to the divisions amongst women, this time along racial lines. Many black women argue that liberal, socialist and radical feminists all share racist assumptions and have failed to relate to the specific experiences of black women (for example, Amos and Parmar, 1984).

For reasons such as these we do not believe it appropriate to speak of women as a *class*. The experience of oppression differs for women from different economic classes and racial/ethnic backgrounds. For black women, the oppression of racism may often take precedence over their oppression as women, or they may choose to organize separately as black women, thus struggling around gender issues within their own community, rather than as part of an all-embracing women's movement.

Nevertheless, despite all these divisions and differences, women do share certain common gender interests which have been largely ignored by the male left and labour movement. Without an autonomous women's movement, women's interests would not get the little attention they do.

We believe that the socialist feminist analysis is most satisfactory in allowing us to explore women's common as well as their contradictory interests. We have found the work of Hartmann and Eisenstein particularly fruitful. It enables us to grapple with the many ways in which capitalism shapes women's position in society, yet also leaves space for us to see how men and women's interests may be in conflict, since men's power in society is neither wholly reducible to, nor necessarily in harmony with, the interests of capital.

We are not arguing that there can be no relations of mutual aid or solidarity between men and women. These can, of course, exist at an individual level. Similarly men and women often join together in collective action around issues which affect them both. Nevertheless, women need an autonomous movement which is independent of other organizations because men and women's interests are often in conflict, and men as a group cannot be relied upon to support women if as a result they would lose some of their privileges. We do not, therefore, agree with Michele Barrett that men are not privileged by the present sexual division of labour in the home. Men do, it is true, have difficult demands placed on them in their role as breadwinner: but in return they have gained a position of power within the home which also enables them to dominate the world outside the home. Their struggle to confine women to the home suggests that, until now, whatever the contradictions facing men, they have as a group tended to favour the *status quo*. As Janet Radcliffe Richards points out:

> Men who think the male role a heavy burden should be rushing to embrace feminism. Since, however, we seem in no danger of being submerged in seas of recruits, and since the average complainer about the male role would not change places with his wife or secretary for anything, we are entitled to suspect that the male role is not as burdensome as some men would have us think. (Richards, 1982, p. 331.)

7 Capitalism patriarchy and the State

Having argued for an approach which sees women's oppression as being shaped by capitalism and by patriarchal relations, we shall conclude by analysing in greater detail how the interests of capital and of men relate to each other and to the State.

The relationship between capitalism and patriarchy is complicated and contradictory. Capital undoubtedly benefits from women's unpaid labour in the home, since without it, the costs of workers' upkeep and hence their wages would, other things being equal, be higher. On the other hand, capital benefits from women's role as a reserve army of labour – a flexible workforce which can be taken on in times of expansion, and reduced during slumps. More recently, technological change has led some industries to take on 'unskilled' women workers in preference to 'skilled' men. Massey and Morgan, (1982), for example document this process in the footwear industry. Once again, capital benefits from the gender role system which casts women in the role of a secondary workforce. On the other hand, the increase in the number of women workers has the potential to undermine certain aspects of patriarchy, since it brings more women into the traditionally male world of the trade union movement, and gives women greater economic independence.

As systems of social relationships, therefore, capitalism and patriarchy are not necessarily mutually reinforcing. Indeed the relationship between them can be seen as one of conflict and accommodation. Thus we cannot assume that the action of the state when it reinforces women's dependency can be explained as a *direct* response to the needs of capitalism.

A more fruitful approach to understanding policies towards women is to see the state as reinforcing women's position in the home because it helps alleviate various political, administrative and fiscal problems confronting the State. Such problems may be partly – but by no means exclusively – attributable to the constraints imposed on the state by the capitalist economy. In the first place, women's unpaid work as carers saves the Treasury billions of pounds of public expenditure each year. This is of increasing significance because of what has been referred to as the tendency of the modern state towards 'fiscal crisis' – the gap between public expenditure and the politically and economically feasible level of tax revenues. This gap can lead to budget deficits, high government borrowing and inflation – all potent sources of political instability in capitalist democracies. We can thus well understand why the capitalist state will not consider paying for all women's unpaid labour in the home.

A second way in which women's work aids the State is in their role as intermediaries between state services and the family. It is women who take children to the doctor, who spend hours in hospital waiting rooms, or discuss 'budgeting difficulties' with housing officers, social security officials and social workers. The time and skill women must devote to this task has increased as social services have grown, and become more complex, specialized and professionalized. Laura Balbo has described women's role as a 'patchwork strategy': they piece together the different state services by acting as a single reference point between the family and the State, increasing the efficiency of state services, and compensating for their 'inhumanity, carelessness and impersonality'. (Balbo, 1981, p. 7.)

Third, we must look at the role of ideology in explaining why the State and political parties promote the ideal of the bourgeois family. This may take several forms. In the first place, Barrett and McIntosh refer to the 'familialisation' of state policies, whereby large scale issues are presented as if they were day-to-day family problems: planning public expenditure is likened to balancing the family budget; workers in a large firm are all 'one big family'. In the process, policies are popularized, and impersonality and incomprehension replaced by a warm, cosy glow.

If familialization is to be successful it must connect with

popular pro-family sentiments. It cannot just be foisted on an unreceptive population. Clearly, the family *is* popular and as a result alternative forms of care for dependants are seen as second best. On the other hand, family values are not promoted *simply* because they are popular. Family values involve putting private life and the interests of immediate kin before public life and allegiance to larger social groups – be they workers, other women or fellow political activists. Family values underpin the depoliticization of social life: it is better to be at home than attend a public meeting; it is better to buy your own home, and spend your evenings doing D-I-Y than join a tenants' association.

A final reason why state policies are sexist lies in the policy making process itself. Men dominate this process whether as politicians, civil servants, or representatives of the major interest groups to which the government feels it must listen. Male domination is the norm whether we are looking at the representatives of capital, or of labour. Policy making thus becomes a process of conflict and accommodation between dominant and subordinate men, a process from which women are largely excluded.

For all these reasons, the State has played a role in promoting the bourgeois family both through reinforcing dominant ideologies about the family and women's role, and through framing social policies on the assumption that women perform unpaid labour in the home and are economically dependent on men. In the next three chapters we shall examine in more detail the manner in which this occurs.

4

Education

Although teachers do not think their pay is very good it does not seem too bad to me and as I hope to get married at a fairly young age this makes the problem less important. Teaching has advantages such as the long holidays and being able to go back to work once one's children are of school age. . . . In teaching one can work part-time which would leave ample time for the normal duties of a mother and housewife.

(From 'My Future Career' by Peggy Foster – aged 14. Written for an English class of a Girls' Grammar School, 1966)

Socialization and women's inequality

It is not difficult for feminists to find evidence that men and the state espouse and attempt to enforce an ideology of gender based on the central assumption that women's primary role is that of unpaid homemakers, mothers and carers. What is more problematic for feminists is why so many women voluntarily perform these roles and, in some cases, defend them vehemently. One key way in which feminists have attempted to explain this phenomenon is by researching the process through which most girls and boys come to acquire strong stereotypical gender roles. Indeed some feminists see socialization as the primary determinant of women's unequal position in society. (See for example Belotti, 1975, p. 13.)

Researchers have clearly demonstrated that the socialization of girls into traditional female roles begins virtually at birth (future research may well discover that parents who know the sex of a foetus begin that socialization process before birth) and that very strong gender roles are well established before children start school. Feminists, partly in an attempt to prove that women are not biologically very different from men, have fully explored the primary role played by parents in the socialization of their children into distinct gender roles.

Sue Sharpe reports the findings of one study of how parents treated children between one and five years of age which found that mothers made more fuss over the appearance of their baby daughters; parents inadvertently focused their children's attention on gender 'appropriate' objects and activities such as dolls for girls and cars for boys; the language parents used to their children, especially when praising or blaming them, differed according to the sex of the child (girls were praised for being 'helpful', boys for being 'brave'); finally, girls were expected to help with domestic chores far more than boys. (Sharpe, 1976.)

One criticism which feminists themselves have made of the dominant perspective of academic women's studies both in Britain and the USA on the socialization of girls into stereotyped gender roles is that this perspective sees sex-role socialization as something which is transmitted to passive recipients. An alternative approach to an understanding of the process by which adult sexual identities are formed, is to stress the active participation of small children in the acquisition of a strong gender identity (see A. Kelly, 1981, pp. 73–83).

Some feminists have developed psychoanalytic ideas to explain why women continue to perform so many 'labours of love' within the family. Juliet Mitchell took a new look at Freudian theories from a feminist perspective in an attempt to provide a more complex understanding of children's acquisition of masculine and feminine identities. Mitchell's *Psychoanalysis and Feminism* (1974) provides a theoretical account of the development of femininity and 'womanhood' based on psychoanalytic concepts. This work has played a key role in the formation of specifically feminist psychoanalytical theories of femininity. Nancy Chodorow has also drawn on a Freudian account of personality development to explain why women continue to be more nurturant than men but she links this account to the social fact that children are predominantly cared for by their mothers. This leads to babies of both sexes forming primary emotional bonds with their mother rather than their father, and leads women (and not men) to seek to recreate the mother role themselves. Chodorow's complex theory has implications for social policy since it implies that: 'the key to rupturing existing gender relations lies in the creation of new patterns of parenting in which men participate equally.' (Nava, 1983, p. 97.)

While the development of explicitly feminist psychoanalytical theories of women's emotional development may eventually prove to have some liberating potential for all women, we must be careful not to overemphasize women's psychological make-up in our explanation of why women continue to be self-sacrificing lovers, wives, mothers and daughters. We must also explore the economic and social structures which push women into particular familial roles. As Hilary Graham has pointed out:

> A theoretical model which explains women's predisposition to care in psychological terms inevitably masks the possibility that it is not a product of an enduring feminine personality but results from the particular way in which reproduction (in its broadest sense) is organised in our society ... women's dependent status is determined by economic as well as psychic forces. (Graham, 1983, p. 21)

Graham suggests that feminists seeking to understand women's caring role need to combine and utilize both psychological studies which explain what caring means to women in essentially emotional terms, and social policy studies, particularly those by marxist–feminist writers, which emphasize the economic and political factors which push women into dependent, caring roles. (See chapter 6.)

Feminists do not claim that either the dominant ideology of women's role or the material conditions faced by women are primarily the results of a sexist education system. Most feminists, as we have pointed out, emphasize the primacy of socialization within the family, particularly in relation to the development of strong gender roles in pre-school children. They also acknowledge that even while attending school most boys and girls are strongly influenced by extra curricular activities, such as watching television and reading magazines, and by their peer groups and their parents. Although children spend approximately 15,000 hours in school from the ages of five to sixteen they spend many more hours out of school, and even during lessons many children may be paying little attention to the messages their teachers are attempting to convey. Nevertheless, in their attempts to explain why women continue to fulfil the subordinate roles which men and the state delineate for them, feminists do place some of the blame on the state education system.

In 1975 the Sex Discrimination Act made it illegal to deny an individual access to education on the grounds of their sex. Henceforth, it was illegal for schools to deny a girl access to any particular subject (apart from sports) or for universities to operate overt quota systems which restricted the proportion of female entrants to medicine or any other discipline. Yet feminists continue to argue that the education system as a whole discriminates against girls and contributes to the subordination of adult women. In 1983, for example, Michelle Stanworth agreed that 'progress has been made towards overcoming gender inequality in schools' but insisted 'it must be said with equal emphasis that there is still a long way to go'. (Stanworth, 1983, p. 7.)

Feminist empirical research into the various processes by which educational institutions reinforce women's unequal position in society is now extensive and feminist theories which attempt to explain the findings of this research are becoming increasingly sophisticated. As feminists have developed divergent views on the fundamental causes of continuing sex discrimination within the education system, debates and controversies within the feminist movement have multiplied. Early feminist research which tended to portray girls as passive recipients of an all pervasive educational sexism is now widely regarded as simplistic, although some radical feminists still regard male dominated education, despite some superficial changes, as so intrinsically patriarchal and oppressive as to be unassailable. (See chapter 9.) In this chapter we will simply attempt, whilst acknowledging the growing complexities of the debate, to identify and elaborate the major common themes of feminist critiques of the education of girls.

According to feminists the education system not only reflects strong societal pressures towards unequal adult gender roles but actually reinforces them. Educational institutions continue to prepare girls for unequal female adult roles in three key ways. First, girls, particularly working-class girls, still emerge from their education with less useful and lucrative qualifications than their male counterparts, and are thus prepared (in both senses of the word) to accept less well paid less secure and less powerful positions in the labour market. Second, girls continue to learn from their educational experiences that they are destined to find fulfilment as wives and mothers as much as, if not more than, as workers. Third, girls, particularly girls in mixed classes, learn that their needs and abilities are subordinate, and should be subordinate, to the needs and abilities of boys. We will now explore how post-war educational policies and the day-to-day experiences of girls in schools both contribute to this preparation of girls for unequal adult roles.

Post-war education policies

Despite the highly visible presence of a very few influential female policy makers – most notably perhaps Margaret Thatcher and Shirley Williams who have both been Secretaries of State for Education – women have never participated fully in the decision-making processes of the educational world. As in all other spheres of public life, where the power is women are absent. Women predominate only at the bottom rungs of the educational career ladder. The very title 'Dinner Lady' speaks for itself, and most educational institutions are kept spick and span by a low paid all female workforce under the supervision of male caretakers. Women form the majority of the teaching staff in most schools but they are clustered at the bottom end of the power hierarchy and the pay structure. In 1979 women made up 74 per cent of teachers in junior with infant schools but only 26 per cent of the heads. In the secondary sector women held 60 per cent of scale 1 posts (lowest level grade), 32 per cent of deputy headships and 16 per cent of headships. (DES, 1981.) Of all full-time teaching and research staff in universities in 1979, 14 per cent were women. Whilst women made up 15 per cent of lecturers they made up only 6 per cent of senior lecturers and readers and 3 per cent of professors. (EOC, 1981a.)

Thus women play a major role in actually teaching boys and girls at least until they are sixteen, but it is men who hold most positions of power within the school system. Similarly, men dominate local and central government both as politicians and as top level civil servants and administrators. Another clear example of how women have played only a minor role in educational decision making since the Second World War is the low proportion of women on the major post-war government committees and quangos in the education field. The influential Robbins Committee of 1963 on Higher Education, for example, had a mere 17 per cent female membership. (Byrne, 1978.)

Given the general lack of women politicians it is hardly surprising that women have played such a minor role in the politics of education. But what influence have men's educational policies had on the education of girls in the second half of the twentieth century? In Britain, politicians have – at least until very recently – consistently claimed that what actually goes on within schools, what is taught and how it is taught, is a professional matter in which politicians as amateurs in educational matters should not and therefore do not interfere. (In line with this strong tradition the Sex Discrimination Act does not 'interfere' with the content of the school curriculum but restricts its area of concern to organizational issues.)

Traditionally the role of central government in relation to the British state education system has been to set only very broad policy guidelines and then to work in partnership with local authorities and the teaching profession in implementing these guidelines. But this does not mean that post-war governments have had no influence over the state education system. In recent decades central governments have initiated several major policy changes in education such as the rapid expansion of the university system in the 1960s and the introduction of comprehensive secondary schools in the late 1960s and 1970s. Both of these major policy changes stemmed – at least in part – from a concern to expand educational opportunities but in neither case did policy makers pay any serious attention to the issue of gender inequalities in education. This is hardly surprising since throughout the 1950s and 1960s educational policy makers supported the notion that education for girls should be different from that provided for boys. Middle-class girls were to be prepared for a dual role as career women and wives and mothers, whilst for working-class girls the emphasis was firmly on preparation for housekeeping and motherhood. (See Arnot, 1983.) Probably the most notorious (in feminist circles) exponent of this 'separate but equal' approach to the education of girls was John Newsom, who in the early 1960s, chaired the influential government committee on the educational needs of average and below average secondary school pupils. In 1948 Newsom claimed that the 'mission of women' was 'to create men and women' both 'physically, mentally and spiritually' and to 'civilise men and thus preserve civilisation'.

According to Newsom education for girls must be designed to help women fulfil their natural role as wives and mothers. Therefore, the curriculum for girls should be designed around 'the home itself'.

Arithmetic concerns household accounts, cookery, furnishing costs and the garden, all involving the basic processes in a wide variety of measures, mensuration, the reading of instruments, percentages and graphs. This is about all the mathematics most girls will ever need. . . . (Newsom, 1948, p. 120.)

Newsom was also particularly keen on ensuring that girls learnt culinary skills:

Somewhere in the curriculum . . . the basic domestic skills should be learned or at least refurbished . . . no girl should be content to accept the responsibility of running a home without the minimum standard and no man in his senses should endanger his comfort and digestion by allowing her to use him as a domestic guinea-pig. (Newsom, 1948, p. 126.)

Given Newsom's strong views on women's proper role in life it is hardly surprising to read in The Newsom Report of 1963 entitled 'Half our Future' that for girls, 'there is a group of interests relating to what many, perhaps most of them would regard as their most important vocational concern, marriage'. (DES, 1963, p. 37), and that 'since caring for the sick and elderly is commonly a woman's responsibility' a course for older girls 'built around broad themes of home making' might include 'home nursing and errands of service to old people in the neighbourhood'. (DES, 1963, p. 137.) However, perhaps some advance had been made between 1948 and 1963 since the report did suggest that some homemaking courses 'could usefully be designed for mixed groups of boys and girls more often than they are'. (DES, 1963, p. 137.)

The Conservative Government which came to power in 1970 gave very low priority to women's education despite the rise of a feminist movement in Britain. Ironically, it was a female Secretary of State for Education, Margaret Thatcher, who in reply to criticism that schools were doing nothing to encourage more girls to take up science subjects, argued in 1973 that if girls chose not to do science that was not an educational problem and went on to suggest that, 'in view of the great debate for relevance as far as education is concerned, there would seem to be some sense in most girls doing some of the domestic science subjects and there is not the time for everything on the curriculum'. (Thatcher, 1973, p. 38.)

Margaret Thatcher also argued strongly that there was no scope for anti-discrimination legislation in the field of education and her strong views were partly responsible for the exclusion of education and training from the Conservative Government's green paper on sex discrimination which was published in 1973.

Nevertheless by the mid-1970s – when a growing feminist
campaign about gender inequalities in society which included a
strong critique of sexist education systems began to have some
impact in political and other circles – gender inequalities did
begin to be placed on the political agenda. In 1975, for example,
the DES carried out a survey of curricular differences for boys
and girls in secondary schools which revealed the extent of the
problem. The DES survey found that, for example, 28 per cent of
mixed schools encouraged early specialization in either arts or
science subjects (feminists need not be told which block of
options the great majority of girls 'chose'), and 25 per cent of
fourth and fifth form girls in mixed schools were not offered the
option of taking physics whereas only 9 per cent of boys were not
offered physics. (DES, 1975). It was partly due to pressure from
feminists who claimed that such statistics proved that the
education system was not providing equal opportunities for girls
that the Sex Discrimination Act of 1975 did include a section on
discrimination in schools and other educational institutions.

Even liberal feminists have admitted that 'the education system
is notoriously resistant to legislation' and feminists of all political
persuasions have pointed out a number of specific weaknesses in
the clauses of the 1975 Act which covered education. It is
particularly difficult for parents to use the law to enforce a
complaint about discrimination against their daughter in a
particular school or education authority. Parents will naturally be
worried about coming into direct conflict with those responsible
for their children's education but even if they are prepared to run
this risk, the legal procedure they would have to follow is neither
simple nor cost free. Unlike cases of discrimination in
employment there are no special tribunals to deal with complaints
about discrimination against female pupils or students, and if the
complaint is not satisfactorily dealt with by the education
authorities the complainant must take her case to a county court.
But taking a complaint through the complex British legal system
can be both daunting and costly – since unsuccessful
complainants may have to pay their own legal costs. Since 1975
only two complaints of discrimination against female pupils have
reached the county court, and one of these failed (see Coote and
Campbell, 1982, p. 121).

There are two possible interpretations of the lack of court cases
in response to the education clauses of the 1975 Act. The EOC
claims that if a complaint reaches the stage of coming before a
county judge, the EOC has failed to do its job successfully, by
ensuring that all complaints are amicably and informally resolved

by the educational authorities concerned. However, there is an alternative interpretation of the lack of court cases under the education sections of the 1975 Act. According to critics of the EOC, it has been far too soft on blatant discrimination in the educational field and has weakened the 1975 Act significantly by failing to ensure that its educational provisions are legally enforced. (See, for example, Coote and Campbell, 1982 p. 123.)

Since 1975 most government documents and directives on education have paid at least some attention to the problem of sex discrimination. In 1981, for example, the government discussion document 'A Framework for the School Curriculum' stated:

> Special consideration should be given by both authorities and schools to the curricular needs of ethnic minorities, the handicapped, the less able and gifted, and to the avoidance of discrimination between the sexes. This last point, is not met simply by making particular subjects and options formally open to boys and girls on equal terms; it is important that the educational and career implications of particular choices should be made clear, and efforts made to prevent traditional differences in the education of boys and girls exercising too strong an influence.

At first sight this commitment to equality is a major advance on the absence of any concern over gender inequalities in pre-1975 policy statements. However, we must examine this new commitment in the context of the Conservative Government's overall educational and social objectives. Even taken on its own, as David points out this 'commitment' to equality between the sexes 'was very muted' (David, 1983). No definition was given to the efforts which should be made to prevent traditional differences continuing, no strategies were outlined for overcoming sex discrimination in schools and finally the precise commitment given was not to equality but only to ensuring that traditional inequalities should not continue to be 'too strong'. Moreover, this commitment to women's equality is in stark contrast to the practical effects on women's educational opportunities of the Conservative Government's education cuts. Many local education authorities, desperately trying to meet central government's tighter and tighter financial constraints, have made deep cuts into adult education provision, and women just happen to be the largest consumers of adult education. The virtual ending in many areas of discretionary grants for further education courses has also severely restricted women's post-school educational opportunities. Severe cuts in university funding meanwhile have dramatically increased competition for university places at a time when, as the Government itself has at last admitted, demand from mature women is rising significantly. Finally, cuts in state nursery care have made it particularly difficult for less well-off women with small children to pursue any form of full-time education.

Miriam David has contrasted the Conservative Government's statements on reducing sex inequalities in schools not only with its educational cuts but also with its other educational objectives. In particular, she highlights the Government's insistence that 'preparation for parenthood and family life' should become 'essential constituents' of the school curriculum. David concludes that the Government is only committed to equality between men and women who have no family responsibilities.

> Otherwise, this pious wish to eradicate sex differences in curricular offerings would run directly counter to its efforts to ensure the teaching of a broad spectrum of moral education, emphasising parental responsibilities in society. The root notion of the family to be used in these latter subjects is patriarchal. ... Woman's main roles, through marriage, are as economically dependent on her husband and as a housewife, caring for both husband and children. In this family model women are, by virtue of their work within the family as both wives and mothers, effectively excluded from equal participation in the labour force. (David, 1983, p. 153.)

In 1982, Dr Rhodes Boyson, then Minister of State for schools, pronounced that women teachers who left their jobs to have a baby should be encouraged to stay at home and educate their own children by a state handout of £800 per annum. (*Daily Express* 4 November 1982.) Public pronouncements such as this certainly suggest that David's critique of the Conservative Government's commitment to sex equality in schools is not simply feminist sour grapes. But however much the Thatcher Government might wish to impose a particular curricular agenda on state schools, its detailed curricular proposals would be very costly to implement and there is no evidence to suggest that the government is as yet prepared to make such a controversial move. According to David the Government's stand on the schools' curriculum is primarily 'moral exhortation' 'and in all probability, impossible to implement' (David, 1983).

Whilst a particularly right-wing government has been altering both the ideological and the financial climate in which the state education system operates, some left-wing local education authorities, notably ILEA, have begun to play an active role in combating sex discrimination in their schools and have set up a number of promising initiatives designed to tackle this practice. What long-term effects such initiatives will have on girls' educational experiences remains to be seen. At this stage, we can only suggest that at a time of severe financial restraints, it would seem unlikely that a few committed local education authorities will be able to secure any general or significant changes within the state school system as a whole.

The schools and gender inequalities

During the 1970s feminists mounted a campaign to remove overt discrimination against girls from the British education system. Today most feminists are no longer solely concerned with overt forms of discrimination, such as the effective exclusion of girls from certain traditionally male subjects. They are also highly critical of what has become known as the hidden curriculum which includes both the hidden messages conveyed through school textbooks and other teaching materials and all interactions between teachers and pupils, many of which are not directly related to the teaching of a specific subject. Feminist research into the hidden curriculum in schools has highlighted both the continuance of some overt sexism and the prevalence among teachers of more implicitly sexist assumptions about female pupils and their future role in life. These assumptions appear to be held by both male and female teachers, many of whom claim to be concerned to provide genuine equality of educational opportunity to all their pupils regardless of their class, race or sex.

Despite the Sex Discrimination Act, overt discrimination against girls cannot be dismissed as no longer an issue. In 1981 a practising physics teacher explained why girls did not do well in his subject thus:

It is a fact that most girls have not the type of mind that faces a problem nor reasons well from given data – not even my star girls who got as far as Oxford and/or Cambridge and to a first and a Ph.D. in one case. Even this girl just could not compare with her boy rivals but she took the subject further and at a university where standards were lower. (Kelly, 1981, p. 258.)

In 1978 *Spare Rib* reported the experiences of a group of schoolgirls whose history master told them 'how clever Hitler was to stop all married women from working because it solved unemployment'. (*Spare Rib*, 1978, p. 7.)

The same master claimed that the results of one history test in which the boys – on average – scored slightly higher than the girls 'proved that men are superior to women'. Overt sexism of the crude type displayed above *may* now play only a minor role in the perpetuation of sexually discriminatory practices within educational institutions. However, studies of the interaction between teachers and the boys and girls in their classes have found that many teachers may be reinforcing sex-stereotypes by their instinctively different treatment of the two sexes. Research in nursery classes has found teachers praising little girls for looking pretty or wearing nice clothes whilst admonishing girls for any type of aggressive behaviour which they tolerate or even openly admire in the boys. One Italian study of the interaction between nursery teachers and their pupils reported a teacher giving the following instructions to little girls, 'Go and take care of your little brother who's crying and wipe his nose', 'There are some construction pieces left under Giagio's desk, Antonietta will you put them away?' (Belotti, 1975 p. 134). The researcher commented on these instructions: 'For a teacher to tell little boys to do similar services for little girls is ... inconceivable. ... One doesn't ask little boys to wipe their little sister's noses, clean up for them or tie their shoelaces.' (Belotti, 1975 p. 134.)

The researcher also observed that even very small boys actively resisted being helpful in the nursery classroom and that the teachers were not prepared to confront them about this. She concluded: 'Women are conditioned to like placing themselves at the service of men. For the conditioning to bear fruit it must begin early. In the family it starts at an extremely young age. It is then reinforced and stabilised in the nursery school.' (Belotti, 1975, p. 131.)

Feminist research into the interactions between British primary school teachers and their pupils has uncovered a very similar pattern of gender differences. In 1978, for example, Byrne reported the following remarks from primary school teachers:

'There's a good girl to help teacher. Such a helpful child, she always offers to put the toys away. ... Gillian do you really want to go out in all that mud – why don't you help me tidy away the crayons?'
'There's a brave boy, Bobby, real boys don't cry. Big boys

don't show when they're afraid. Well done Ian (he's a born leader you know, always has his team ready first).' (Byrne, 1978, p. 84.)

Researchers have found that primary school teachers not only encourage 'normal' boys and girls to adopt different types of behaviour in the classroom, they also strongly discourage what they regard as 'abnormal' behaviour by pupils of either sex. Clarricoates found that a seven-year-old called Michael who loved to play with dolls really worried the teaching staff at his primary school. His classroom teacher on reading his 'diary' for the morning which read 'One Saturday I helped my Mum bake a cake and I made a dress for my doll' asked him despairingly 'Couldn't you play football or something?' She then took away the doll he was clutching and offered him 'Action Man' as a suitable substitute. Michael's headteacher 'a kind, progressive woman' suspected that he had 'feminine genes' and commented that if he was not 'cured' by the time he left school the only solution to his 'problem' would be to enter the world of arts, drama or music where 'that kind of behaviour' would be much more acceptable (Clarricoates, 1980, p. 35).

Feminists do not claim that girls receive a poor formal education in primary schools. In terms of academic achievement girls actually do better, on average, at primary school level than boys. Ironically this may be partly due to teachers urging little girls to adopt feminine virtues. Boys appear to be allowed to be more disruptive and inattentive at primary school level, while girls are more strongly encouraged to be helpful and obedient. Some American educationalists have even argued that too many female teachers in primary schools create a feminine environment which discriminates against little boys and ought therefore to be modified. Feminists argue on the other hand that the educational advantages of helpful obedient girls are very short-lived and that by the time they have left primary school girls have learnt, at least partly from their schooling, particular types of behaviour, and particular images of the adult world, which lead them ultimately into traditionally 'feminine' and therefore unequal adult roles. Feminist research has also suggested that at secondary schools teachers are less likely to reward the 'feminine virtues' of neatness and unquestioning obedience, and are much more likely to praise pupils for the more 'masculine virtues' of intellectual questioning and experimentation.

It is while they are at secondary school that many girls still 'choose' educational paths which lead into traditionally female qualifications and careers. Since 1975 some education experts insist that if girls still choose to take cookery rather than computing science, it can only be because girls are naturally better at some forms of activity than at others. In 1981, for example, J. Gray, a fellow of University College Oxford, argued that women are genetically worse – on average – than men at spatial tasks and therefore at mathematical and scientific subjects. The conclusion he drew from this 'scientific' evidence on women's innate handicap in relation to certain school subjects was that nothing needed to be done to remedy sex differences in science achievement: 'It is with a clear conscience . . . that we may welcome the different patterns of intellectual abilities shown by the sexes as an addition to diversity in a society which badly needs it.' (Gray, 1981, p. 52.)

Most feminists do *not* welcome such 'diversity'. Dale Spender suggests that women ought to be extremely suspicious whenever powerful men define women as naturally bad at those very subjects which give most power and prestige to those who are naturally good at them (Spender, 1980). Whereas radical feminists such as Dale Spender blame women's continuing lack of success in traditionally male subjects almost exclusively on men's domination of all educational institutions, most feminists accept that the factors behind girls' continued absence in certain fields of endeavour are extremely complex. Alison Kelly, who has been closely involved in action research designed to encourage more schoolgirls to take science subjects, gives three key explanations for the female drop-out rate from scientific study: girls' lack of confidence which leads them to see science subjects as too difficult for them, the masculine image of science both as a school subject and as a career, and the impersonal approach to science, which seems to have little to do with 'caring' for and about people. Kelly believes that, while these three factors cannot be divorced from the image of science and the ideology of women as carers which are dominant in society as a whole, schools and, in particular, some male teachers, do still play a part in turning girls off traditionally male subjects (Kelly, 1982). Research within schools has revealed, for example, that maths and physics teachers, the majority of whom are male, continue to gear their lessons to the boys in their classes. In 1981 a sixteen-year-old school leaver wrote about her science education: 'If we did an experiment it would always be the boys who would do them, the teacher would say that the boys should do the experiment because he must have thought the girls were stupid . . .' (Kelly, 1981, p. 234).

Some science teachers also appear to underestimate girls' scientific abilities and to convey these prejudices to their pupils. A few male science teachers may even deliberately try to scare off girls from taking their classes. One female physics teacher has reported.

> Some masters have told me that they deliberately frighten off the girls – especially in the first term of the sixth form – by making the work difficult. Girls who are more conscientious and less confident drop out, and then they revert to the normal standard of work. (Kelly, 1981, p. 258.)

Male science teachers are by no means the only secondary school teachers who have been found to favour the boys. Research into pupil–teacher interaction within secondary schools has revealed that girls are ignored and/or stereotyped by teachers of both sexes. Michelle Stanworth's research based on detailed individual interviews with teachers and pupils in seven 'A' level classes found that male teachers in particular kept the girls in their classes at a distance and gave more individual attention to boys, but that female teachers were also particularly responsive to the needs of male pupils. Both male and female teachers got to know the boys more quickly and chose them as the pupils to whom they were most attached and about whom they were most concerned. The teachers expected the girls, even those with outstanding academic records, to enter 'subordinate and conventionally feminine occupations' and to take on domestic commitments as well as a job or a career. Stanworth concluded from this research evidence:

> Even when girls are performing more successfully than boys, it is boys who stand out in co-educational classes. Girls appear to exist on the periphery of classroom life; their marginalisation in the classroom, and the lesser attention they receive from teachers, results in girls appearing to others – and, more importantly, to themselves – as less capable than they really are. (Stanworth, 1983, p. 52.)

Similarly Dale Spender's research into the interaction between teachers and pupils in mixed secondary school classes demonstrated that even teachers who explicitly aimed to spend an equal amount of time with boys and girls in their classes, actually spent considerably more time interacting with boys. Moreover, Spender found that when feminist teachers tried to give more of their attention to girls, boys quickly protested that they were being unfair, even though in practice the boys were still getting nearly two-thirds of these teachers' attention. (Spender, 1982.)

Feminists do not place all the blame for sex-stereotyping in schools on teachers. Research has shown that pupils are also presented with stereotypical gender roles from the educational materials used in schools. Lobban, having surveyed the reading schemes used in primary schools in the mid-1970s found that they presented children with a picture of women which focused almost exclusively on their role as mothers and housewives. Little girls were pictured helping Mummy with household tasks or standing passively by as their brothers performed daring feats. Lobban concluded from her research that the world these reading schemes depicted was 'not only sexist it was more sexist than present reality and in many ways totally foreign to the majority of children who do have at least some experience of cross-sex activities'. (Lobban, 1976, p. 42.)

Feminists have also explored the hidden curriculum of secondary school textbooks and have discovered that even in subjects at which girls traditionally do well such as history and home economics, the picture of women and their role in society which is conveyed is still strongly stereotyped. Feminist historians have pointed out that the inclusion of women in new history textbooks is hardly a major advance for feminism if women are predominantly portrayed as someone's wife, mother or housekeeper. According to Turnball *et al.*, 'For any period in human history you can find a text which states in one way or another that "a woman's place was in the home".' (Turnbull, Pollock and Bruley, 1983, p. 152.)

Since home economics has always been traditionally geared to preparing women for their home-making role, we should not be too surprised to read in a 1964 textbook entitled *Setting Up Your Own Home* that 'A woman's great strength lies in her truly feminine qualities and skills as a homemaker for her man and her children. This is a role which cannot be reversed.' (Wynn, 1983, p. 202.)

Feminists may be disappointed to learn, however, that a textbook published in 1975 emphasizes that 'Running a home is not just one of the sacrifices a girl must make in order to gain a house and a husband but on the contrary it can have a positive aspect needing intelligence, creativity, imagination and organisation.' (Wynn, 1983, p. 202.)

We should not ignore the work which many teachers and educationalists have put into producing less-sexist teaching materials in the last ten years. One home economics textbook now advises pupils that when they marry they must 'try to share all the household duties fairly and happily and this includes the kitchen . . .' (Wynn, 1983, p. 205).

Despite some changes, however, most school textbooks have yet to be changed significantly, in response to the feminist challenge. For example, several studies of the sex of people in illustrations of contemporary physics and chemistry textbooks have found a ratio of approximately four men to every one woman. Moreover, in 1980, Walford found that the minority of pictures which did feature women showed them 'pushing prams, blowing bubbles, cooking, working as radiographers or nurses, being patients, looking sexy, amazed or frightened or simply doing "silly" things'. (Walford, 1980) – hardly the type of role models which would encourage girls to pursue high-flying scientific careers! Meanwhile feminist teachers cannot produce enough special non-sexist teaching packs to redress the sexist balance in mainstream textbooks. In 1983, a survey of sexist bias in geography teaching concluded 'There are no non-sexist geography teaching packs yet available . . .' (Larsen, 1983, p. 177).

The conclusion reached by Dale Spender in 1980 on the effects of a sexist schools curriculum are, therefore, unlikely to be outdated:

> The books and materials used within our schools abound in crude and inaccurate images of men and women and are designed to indoctrinate children in sexual inequality . . . from elementary reading schemes to A-level texts, these same biased images proliferate and convey the same sexist message. Image after sexist image functions to convince younger members of society that men and women are different – and unequal – and hence the possibility of choice (of adult roles) is pre-empted. (Spender, 1980, p. 25.)

Discussion

Feminist research into the contemporary education of girls has not revealed any straightforward evidence that all female pupils are being coercively pushed by overtly sexist educational policy makers and teachers into stereotypical gender roles which are then solely responsible for adult women taking unequal low paid jobs and willingly accepting unpaid family duties. Whilst some radical feminists argue that a male dominated process of socialization, both within patriarchal families and within patriarchal educational institutions, is primarily responsible for women's oppression, socialist feminists stress that socialization is only one of the factors which contribute to women's unequal position in society. Socialist feminists also emphasize that the educational experiences of white upper-and middle-class girls are usually far less oppressive than the experiences of girls from working-class and ethnic minority backgrounds. Significant numbers of girls from privileged backgrounds do now achieve very high educational qualifications and use these qualifications to pursue lucrative and powerful careers – albeit less lucrative and less powerful, on average, than their equivalently qualified male counterparts.

Most feminist research into education has focused on the key differences between the educational experiences of all girls in relation to all boys. We would suggest that much more research needs to be done on the particular educational experiences of working-class and black girls. They appear to be much more likely than white middle-class girls to be channelled into subjects such as cookery, mothercare and typing which strongly emphasize their future domestic role and their very limited career options. Black girls, moreover, are still subjected to racism as well as sexism in most British schools and thus suffer a double form of oppression which has not been seriously investigated by white feminist researchers.

Feminist research into education has concentrated on mainstream schooling but those girls identified as delinquent – and it is working-class and black girls who are most likely to gain this label – may be educated in special schools. One study of an approved school for girls suggests that sex stereotyping and sexist forms of socialization may be particularly rife in such schools. Ackland found that all approved schools aimed to train their residents by socializing them into acceptable patterns of behaviour but whereas for boys this meant stressing the importance of desirable work habits, for girls it usually meant learning to cook and sew and to care for a family. Ackland concluded this study:

The traditional stereotype of women's role in society as essentially submissive and non-aggressive and in which child-rearing and caring for a home are regarded as primary obligations, had a strong bearing on what the staff considered to be appropriate and acceptable behaviour for their female charges. (Ackland, 1982, p. 146.)

We must not exaggerate the extent to which working-class and black girls accept the sexist/racist version of their future roles which many schools still present to them. One girl in the approved school discussed above when asked whether the school had helped her, commented: 'No, definitely not. They don't teach you properly ... All you do is cook and needlework.' (Ackland, 1982, p. 120.)

We are also aware that at least some of those girls who emerge from school without any formal educational qualifications and who perceive their future primarily in terms of lovers and mothers may have 'chosen' these roles more because of external influences than because of sexism within the school system. Research has suggested, for example, that some adolescent girls in mixed schools may actively strive to appear less clever than the boys they 'fancy' and may firmly avoid becoming identified with non-feminine subjects such as physics.

Whilst we accept that the socialization of girls does not take place exclusively or even primarily within schools, and that girls are not simply passive recipients of an all-pervasive sexism within educational institutions, we would claim that schools still play some part in preparing girls for their unequal stereotyped adult roles as workers and as wives, mothers and unpaid carers. Many of these women, particularly working class women, who 'choose' to become part-time low paid workers or full-time unpaid carers later find themselves leading unequal, restricted and unfulfilled lives. In the next chapter, we will explore the ways in which doctors and social workers act as agents of social control by advising and even pushing their women clients into these traditional female roles. So we will conclude this chapter with a question. How much harder would doctors and social workers have to push their female clients into traditional female roles if women had not already been softened up to accept their unequal position in society by, amongst other forces, their educational experiences?

5

Welfare professionals and the control of women

In this chapter we will focus on the important role doctors and, to a lesser extent, social workers play in creating, interpreting and attempting to enforce a particular role for women which, we would argue, serves the needs of both men and the capitalist state. We will demonstrate that welfare professionals exercise social control over female welfare clients in two major ways. First, they frequently give advice and sometimes treatment to women which is intended to reinforce women's willingness to perform the roles of submissive wives, lovers, unpaid homemakers, child minders and carers for other dependants such as the frail elderly. Second, they have the power to exercise control over women's access to certain material resources and benefits which women need to control for themselves if they are to gain autonomy over their own lives.

Feminists of different political persuasions strongly disagree over the basic causes of the negative control which welfare professionals exercise over women. (See chapter 8.) The issue of professionalism *per se*, however, has received very little attention from feminists. This omission is unfortunate, and we believe that an explicitly feminist analysis of the role which professionalism itself plays in the conflict between women and the Welfare State will be of use to feminists fighting for change within welfare.

Doctors' control over female sexuality

When contemporary feminists began to assess women's position in both the family and the labour market, many soon reached the conclusion that women would not achieve liberation in either sphere unless they could gain full control over their own reproduction. In 1970, for example, Lucinda Cisler claimed: 'Without the full capacity to limit her own reproduction a woman's other "freedoms" are tantalizing mockeries that cannot be exercised.' (Cisler, 1970, p. 274.)

Free contraception and abortion on demand was one of the original four demands of the British WLM. Feminists now also place considerable emphasis on the oppression of women inherent in sexual relationships defined and delineated by masculine concepts and enforced by male domination. Feminist demands on these two issues have brought them into direct conflict with the medical profession which not only exercises direct control over women's access to abortion and certain types of contraception but also defines and exerts control over female sexuality and reproduction.

Feminist historians have revealed that during the nineteenth century the medical profession played a key role in formulating and propagating scientific myths about women's sexuality and reproductive role. By the latter half of the nineteenth century medical men had created a 'scientific' portrait of woman, or rather of upper- middle-class woman, as a frail sickly creature dominated by her ovaries and destined by nature to be passive, dependent, sexually inactive and above all maternal. Victorian doctors warned women that any attempt to thwart their natural destiny – motherhood – would have disastrous consequences. According to Dr Gardner, for example, writing in 1905, any attempt to prevent pregnancy by using contraception would result in 'moral degradation, physical disability, premature exhaustion and decrepitude'. (Corea, 1977, p. 104.)

In the nineteenth century, doctors' control over women was not restricted to the giving of frightening warnings and pseudo-scientific advice. In their attempts to define and control women's sexuality some doctors treated women, sometimes in the most brutal way, for the illness of sexuality which they called 'nymphomania', 'ovriomania' or 'uterine madness'. Gena Corea has succinctly summed up the effect on upper- and middle-class women of the nineteenth-century medical model of femininity thus:

Women were forced to cripple themselves to fit the medical definition of 'decent women'. If they failed to do so male physicians would do the crippling for them – cutting out their clitorises or ovaries if they exhibited the sexual feelings doctors said they could not have.   (Corea, 1977, p. 111.)

Feminist histories of the treatment of Victorian women by male doctors not only constitute an important antidote to the more conventional view of the rise of professional medicine as a wholly progressive process, but also provide an important insight for contemporary feminist struggles. If we can now see clearly that so much nineteenth-century medicine was a form of social control over women, should we not also question the motives of contemporary medicine towards women? Feminists who have investigated contemporary medical doctrines on the nature of women and their problems have indeed found a strong sexist ideology lying just beneath the surface of medical advice and treatment. They have discovered that whilst some doctors are now far less patriarchal in their attitudes and practices than their Victorian counterparts, many others are still overtly sexist. Moreover, despite the valiant efforts of some feminist doctors and a few male doctors sympathetic to the feminist position, the medical profession as a whole still exercises significant control over women's sexuality and reproductive functions.

Feminist reviews of contemporary medical textbooks show that although the medical model of female sexuality has certainly moved on from the virtually totally sexless ideal woman portrayed in the nineteenth century, contemporary medicine has yet to abandon its presumptuous claim to set a sexual norm for all women and to define female sexuality primarily in relation to men's sexual needs and to the female urge to reproduce. Some contemporary gynaecological texts do now emphasize that women are sexually active and responsive creatures who should be 'helped' to achieve sexual satisfaction. According to *Human Reproduction* published in 1976, for example, 'Under ideal circumstances the sexual capacity of the human female is greater than that of men.' And 'essentially any woman can be brought to orgasm by effective and appropriate stimulation'. (Page, Villee and Villee, 1976, p. 82.)

Other textbooks published in the 1970s, however, still subordinate female sexuality to men's sexual needs. Novak advises, for example, that:

The frequency of intercourse (in marriage) should depend primarily upon the male sex drive. . . . The female should be advised to allow her male partner's sex drive to set their pace and she should attempt to gear hers satisfactorily to his . . . lack of consideration for the male partner's inherent physical drive is a common cause of impotence and reflects an immature attitude of the female who is using her partner for self-gratification. (Novak, Jones and Jones, 1975, p. 421.)

Sir Norman Jeffcoate, a noted (and in feminist circles infamous) British gynaecologist claims in the 1975 edition of his widely used textbook that 'An important feature of sex desire in the man is the urge to dominate the woman and subjugate her to his will: in the woman acquiescence to the masterful takes a high place.' (Jeffcoate, 1975, p. 568.)

In America many women see gynaecologists relatively frequently and may well get direct advice from them on a range of sexual problems. In Britain women are more often advised by their GPs. Since medical consultations are usually private we know very little about the day-to-day relationship between doctors and their female patients. Most feminists, however, have heard many horror stories about the sexist and judgmental sexual advice doled out by GPs to their female patients. One of the authors of this book was once told by her GP that her pelvic pains were caused by her living in sin with her boyfriend and was advised that the pain would cease if she were to get married and have children. Another source available to feminists is articles and books written by practising GPs. Although we should be careful not to make any sweeping generalizations from a few selected examples, we can at least illustrate that sexism is still overtly displayed by GPs writing about female sexuality.

In 1979 *World Medicine* published an article on 'The Myths of Sexual Medicine' by a Kent GP, who wrote:

A counsellor of my not-too-distant acquaintance provided an example of prescribing one's own opinions as a therapy. A patient with a rather reluctant wife was told that it was time-you-tore-her-knickers-off-and-gave-her-a-darned-good-servicing sort of thing. The advice that he gave to others was hard to visualise in his own relationship . . . though perhaps I prove my point at my own expense, the one thing I always felt might have done him and his wife good was to have her knickers removed forcibly and with some regularity . . . etc., etc. (Richards, 1979, p. 51.)

A 1978 publication which reported a series of discussions held by a group of GPs on the handling of women patients' requests for abortions is replete with sexist remarks, referring for example to a forty-two-year-old female patient as 'mutton dressed up as lamb' and to another female patient as 'overweight, blowsy, not stupid, but apparently feckless'. (Tunnadine and Green, 1978.)

According to Ehrenreich and English the burden of controlling rebellious women is now borne primarily by psychiatrists (Ehrenreich and English, 1973, p. 84). Certainly American feminists have collected a significant amount of evidence on the social control exerted over sexually 'deviant' women by both psychiatrists and psychotherapists. Chesler recounts incidents of women, especially adolescents and wives, being psychiatrically incarcerated during the 1960s for 'promiscuity'. Once in a mental asylum or psychiatric ward, female patients were encouraged to become 'feminine' by paying attention to their appearance and discouraged or prohibited from having lesbian relationships. Ironically, many of the patients Chesler interviewed who were prohibited from any sexual contact with other patients – male or female – reported that they had been propositioned by male members of staff. (Chesler, 1972.)

Unfortunately, there is no British equivalent to Chesler's *Women and Madness*. Nairne and Smith's British study *Dealing with Depression* states: 'Within the therapeutic context of hospital and treatment women are open to all sorts of abuse. We can be (and no doubt are) sexually abused by doctors, therapists, male nurses and male patients.' (Nairne and Smith, 1984, p. 107.) However, the only evidence they produce to back up this statement is taken from an American study, and in the footnotes they comment that 'To our knowledge this has not been "officially" studied in Britain.' Nevertheless, anecdotal evidence strongly suggests that British feminists have no cause to be complacent over the way women are treated within British psychiatric institutions and we would urge British feminist researchers to look more systematically at this aspect of women's medical 'treatment'.

Doctors' control over female reproduction

The nineteenth-century medical profession, as we have noted, condemned any use of contraceptives or abortion mainly on the grounds that they would prevent women from fulfilling their one true mission in life, motherhood. In the late twentieth century the dominant medical ideology of women still portrays them as finding their primary fulfilment in motherhood. In 1976, for example, Walker's gynaecological textbook stated that a woman's first pregnancy represents 'a transition to full womanhood'. (Walker, MacGillivary and MacNaughton, 1976, p. 590.) But despite this ideology many doctors now seem to be concerned to prevent certain types of women from having too many children or – in the worst cases – any children at all.

The medical profession, particularly those working in the NHS, exert a tight control over women's access to certain forms of contraception, such as the pill and to free sterilizations and abortions. Consequently doctors' views on fertility control play an important role in determining women's reproductive choices and experiences. Feminist research suggests that whilst a few doctors may now believe that all women have the right to control their own fertility by the method of their own choice, this is certainly not the dominant medical view.

Many doctors openly advocate the coercive use of contraceptives and sterilization against 'over fertile' Third World women and 'unsuitable' mothers in the advanced world. A survey carried out in America in the late 1970s found that 94 per cent of gynaecologists polled in four major cities favoured compulsory sterilization for welfare mothers with three or more illegitimate children. (Ruzek, 1978, p. 47.)

In 1971, *Shaw's Textbook of Gynaecology* argued that if 'the more intellectual members of the community' continued to practise contraception whilst 'the less intelligent members of the community' continued to produce large numbers of offspring the result would be 'a gradual dilution of the intellectual capacity of the community'. (Howkins and Bourne, 1971, p. 351.) Sir Norman Jeffcoate fully shares this concern over the long-term dangers of voluntary contraception but he does reluctantly admit that compulsory contraception or sterilization is 'at present' wholly contrary to medical ethics. (Jeffcoate, 1975, p. 609.)

Unfortunately, feminist research has revealed that current medical ethics notwithstanding doctors do sometimes sterilize women without obtaining their proper consent. American feminists have documented a significant number of instances in the United States of poor women from ethnic minorities being pressurized into having their tubes tied during the final stages of labour when they were hardly in a position voluntarily to give their informed consent. (Dreifus, 1977.) In Britain a relatively small number of women are sterilized at the time of delivery or during an abortion and in 1975 Sue O'Sullivan stated that the virtually compulsory sterilizations described by the women's movement in America did not seem to exist in Britain. O'Sullivan did claim, however, that in British hospitals some working class women with more than three children were being pressured to have a sterilization thrown in with any gynaecological surgery and that this pressure was greater still on Afro-Caribbean and Asian women. 'Often this is proposed when a mother is attempting to get a National Health abortion – as part of the deal.' (O'Sullivan, 1975.) Jean Aitken-Swan's study of the British medical profession's attitudes towards fertility control provides evidence that at least some doctors in this country favour the sterilization of 'feckless' women. One GP stated that he pushed his 'feckless' patients into sterilization after two children 'for the good of the country as it were', whilst one gynaecologist, but only one out of the thirteen interviewed, spoke of eugenic grounds for sterilization – 'If I've a stupid woman of 22 who's quite inadequate and I have a feeling that from a eugenic standpoint, if nothing else it would be a good thing to sterilise her, I'll do it.' (Aitken-Swan, 1977, p. 157.)

As well as exposing the practice of 'enforced' sterilizations, feminists have also mounted a campaign against the coercive use of the long term injectable contraceptive known as Depo-Provera. They have unearthed a great deal of medical research evidence which suggests that Depo-Provera has many dangerous and unpleasant side-effects. Despite this evidence the manufacturers of Depo-Provera and population control programmers have pushed this form of contraception very hard, particularly in the Third World. British feminists have expressed strong concern about the way in which Depo-Provera has been used in this country. The British campaign against Depo-Provera has found that it has been used on some working-class women but primarily on black women. Cases have been reported to the campaign of women being given the injection without being told what it was. Bengali women in Leeds were told it was a routine post-natal injection. Women in mental hospitals have been told it is a tranquillizer. One Afro-Caribbean teenage girl who had requested a prescription for the pill while she was in hospital for an abortion was given Depo-Provera without her consent whilst she was under anaesthetic. Doctors may claim that they only use Depo-Provera as a last resort on women who are incapable of using any other method of contraception, but the campaign against Depo-Provera strongly rejects this argument, and claims that its use in Britain is primarily as a form of social control directed particularly at ethnic minorities (Berer, 1984).

Ironically, at the same time as some poor women and women from ethnic minorities may face being targeted for compulsory contraception or being pushed into sterilization, married white middle-class women who want to be sterilized, obtain an abortion or simply remain voluntarily childless sometimes face considerable opposition from their doctors. One GP in Aitken-Swan's study stated that he would try to dissuade a young married woman who decided she could not afford another baby from having an abortion whilst another GP simply would not refer a woman who was married and wanted 'a therapeutic abortion of convenience'. (Aitken-Swan, 1977, p. 70.)

Feminists are appalled at the way so many doctors dismiss abortions of which they disapprove as abortions of 'convenience'. Doctors' use of this term strongly suggests that some women who take the very difficult decision to have an abortion do so lightly. There is no empirical evidence to support this view of women's attitudes to abortion. There *is* some evidence that NHS doctors and other medical staff not only loudly express their disapproval of certain abortions but even deliberately punish some women who 'demand' an abortion on the NHS.

Many doctors working in the NHS still seem to make a clear distinction between married women and single women when dealing with requests for abortion. Sally MacIntyre's research into doctors' responses to single pregnant women revealed that both GPs and gynaecologists drew a firm line between patients who might get married and those who were likely to remain single. The doctors all regarded pregnancy amongst married or about to be married women as unproblematic and therefore to be encouraged whereas pregnant women who intended to stay single but pregnant faced considerable pressure from doctors to either have an abortion or to give the baby up for adoption. MacIntyre found that these doctors took little or no account of their patients' own definitions of their situation but rather assumed what their feelings were based on this single/married distinction. (MacIntyre, 1976.)

Doctors and reproductive technology

During the 1970s, as we have just seen, feminists challenged the medical profession's control over women's access to contraceptive and abortion services. A growing number of feminists also expressed deep concern over the damaging physical and psychological effects on women of the ever increasing medicalization of their reproductive lives. Female researchers exposed, for example, a long list of hitherto ignored or suppressed side effects of medically prescribed contraceptives and of high technology obstetric care. They accused a predominantly male medical profession and drugs industry of 'selling' these new benefits to women without warning them of the high price they might have to pay (see for example Corea, 1977, and Dreifus, 1977).

By the early 1980s a new and potentially revolutionary field of medical intervention known as reproductive technology was beginning to attract a very similar range of feminist critiques. The medical techniques subsumed under the label of reproductive technology include *in vitro* fertilization (so called test-tube babies), artificial insemination by donor (AID), genetic engineering and counselling and foetal testing such as amniocentesis (see Arditti *et al.*, 1984, glossary for an explanation of these terms).

The predominantly male scientists and doctors who are perfecting these techniques claim that they hold out the hope of a much better reproductive future for mankind in which all babies will be 100 per cent healthy; all couples who want babies will be able to have them and all babies will be wanted by those who rear them. A vision of a future society in which reproductive technology is used to give human beings and especially women real control and choice over their lives is one shared by some feminists. Both Shulamith Firestone and Marge Piercy have created imaginary future societies in which patriarchy has been overthrown and women use test-tube baby techniques to free themselves completely from the oppression of individual motherhood (Firestone, 1979, Piercy, 1980).

Some women have not waited for the revolution. A few lesbians and single heterosexual women have already established self-help networks which enable them to use the technique of artificial insemination to attempt to conceive without any expert or even male involvement – except as initial sperm donors (see Klein, 1984). Many more women, desperately seeking to have a baby of their own, have willingly turned to the experts for help.

We must emphasize, therefore, that most feminists do not object to new reproductive technology *per se*. We ourselves accept that many infertile women are extremely grateful to those doctors who try to help them by using new and even experimental techniques. We also acknowledge that foetal testing and genetic counselling are regarded by many women as enabling them to exercise more choice and control over their own reproduction. Nevertheless we do share some of the many reservations which feminists are now expressing about the current practice and future possibilities of reproductive technology.

Feminists emphasize that reproductive technology is being developed and utilized within a society which is still very much dominated by men and which clings to a dominant ideology of women as mothers first – if not foremost. Infertile women who desperately seek a 'cure' do not exercise this choice in a social vacuum. The urge towards motherhood may or may not be instinctive. What is clear is that in a society which restricts women's options and continues to emphasize the joys of motherhood, infertile women are likely to feel doubly let down. Doctors cannot of course be held solely responsible for society's attitudes towards infertility, although they have played a significant role in the construction of the dominant ideology of motherhood. Moreover, some feminists argue that the very development of medical treatments for female infertility may in itself reinforce women's role as child bearers (see Albury, 1984).

As well as exploring the social construction of the problem of infertility feminists have asked a number of questions about the medical profession's response to this problem. Why does the medical profession give priority to the development of high technology cures for infertility rather than to the prevention of the rising tide of female infertility? Why have doctors not warned more women of the risk of infertility created by the use of modern contraceptives? What costs do infertile women seeking a medical cure have to bear? Do doctors – who may well believe they are simply responding to a clearcut and urgent medical need – carefully balance the costs of infertility treatments against their benefits? Some feminists have pointed out that the costs of the more complex forms of infertility treatment may include many years of painful debilitating and even humiliating tests and procedures – and that after all that a significant number of infertile women will remain childless (see Rothman, 1984).

At present virtually all of the new reproductive tehniques are firmly in the control of experts and there is no possibility – in the foreseeable future at least – of women using the more complex of these techniques without expert help. The majority view of the medical profession appears to be that they alone should determine which women will gain access to technological conception programmes. In 1983 a report issued by the Royal College of Obstetricians and Gynaecologists, to regulate the practice of *in vitro* fertilization, embryo replacement and embryo transfer in Britain, stated firmly that all these practices were to be guided entirely by the clinical judgment and experience of physicians. The needs and rights of prospective parents – referred to throughout the report as patients – were to be evaluated solely by doctors whose role gave them a special responsibility 'for the welfare of the child thus conceived'. (Hubbard, 1984.) The medical authors of this report concluded that doctors have a natural right to decide which of the many women wanting *in vitro* fertilization would make fit and proper mothers. We are concerned that experts' tight control over access to such treatments may further oppress whole groups of women, including lesbians, mothers living on welfare benefits and women from ethnic minorities all of whom, past and present experience suggests are highly unlikely to be deemed fit and suitable mothers by most welfare professionals. Some feminists have even imagined a horrifying reproductive future in which male experts will designate some women to be egg donors (willingly or unwillingly) others to be ambulatory incubators and yet others as suitable rearers of the resulting babies (Albury, 1984).

Many people – women as well as men – might pour scorn on such an extreme reaction to new medical developments. Doctors may claim that they are simply trying to reduce human misery by helping the infertile and preventing babies being born with severe genetic or other defects. In itself this aim is laudable but feminists have pointed out that in attempting to achieve it doctors do impose certain costs on women. A woman's right to have a baby – now used as a major justification for experimentation on women's bodies – might one day become a woman's overriding duty to submit to whatever new tests or techniques the experts devise in order to ensure perfectly healthy babies. Eventually women may lose the right to refuse certain forms of medical intervention. Some doctors (and lawyers) are now claiming that a well developed foetus is a patient in its own right and that a mother therefore has no right to refuse any intervention which the doctor believes will benefit her foetus. (See Rothman, 1984.) Many people may sympathize with doctors' overriding concern for the foetus but procedures designed to ensure a healthy child are not always totally benign. We are particularly concerned about the possibilities of using foetal testing and other techniques to allow couples to choose the sex of their children. Already some women in India have had to abort a perfectly healthy female foetus after an amniocentesis test has revealed that the desired male child will be a girl. (Roggencamp, 1984.)

In conclusion, we fear that within a patriarchal society the tight control exercised by experts over new reproductive technology may have serious consequences for many women now and in the future. Already doctors are firmly asserting their right to control access to the new techniques and are attempting to outlaw do-it-yourself female solutions to infertility. In the recent scandal over the first commercial surrogate baby to be born in Britain many doctors insisted that surrogacy arrangements could only be contemplated if they were firmly under expert control. There is, therefore, a clear danger that under the laudable guise of extending 'mankind's' ability to have healthy, wanted, well cared for babies the medical profession and the other welfare professionals will further tighten the experts' control over female reproduction.

Doctors and women's caring role

Doctors not only attempt to define and control women's reproductive and sexual lives, they also often attempt to reinforce women's caring role by the advice and treatment which they give to both caring and uncaring patients. Barrett and Roberts found, for example, that the GPs in their study, when consulted by married middle-aged female patients who were suffering from symptoms of stress, anxiety or tiredness, frequently gave them the 'medical' advice that they should give up their jobs. Only very occasionally did a GP tentatively suggest that where both partners were working some of the household tasks might be shared amongst all the members of the family (Barrett and Roberts, 1978). Most housewives and mothers who consult their GP complaining of severe tiredness, anxiety or depression are 'treated' with tranquillizers and anti-depressants. In the early 1980s one woman in five compared to one man in ten was taking tranquillizers, at some time during the course of a year. Major drug companies' advertisements have told GPs that tranquillizers or anti-depressants are the solution to problems such as women living in high rise flats (Tristafen), women being unable to choose between goods in a supermarket (Prothiaden), female students under stress (Tranxene), and the boredom of housework (Limbitrol). Doctors claim to be unaffected by drug advertising but nevertheless continue to give psychotropic drugs to very many female patients. Feminists not only criticize the over prescribing of psychotropic drugs to women on the grounds that these drugs may be addictive and have serious side effects, they also argue that the drugging of so many women should be seen as a form of social control which keeps women passive but does nothing to solve their real problems or to alter the social conditions which are primarily responsible for making many women depressed in the first place.

Even more worrying to feminists than the use of tranquillizers as 'mothers little helpers' are the coercive forms of treatment experienced by some women in psychiatric institutions. Barrett and Roberts reported in 1978 several examples of the British psychiatric system being used to confirm women in their traditional family and domestic roles. They discovered more than one instance where a woman's refusal to do housework had eventually led to hospitalization and ECT. (Barrett and Roberts, 1978.)

Documentary evidence on the use of psychosurgery to control 'deviant' women comes primarily from American researchers. In 1974 Roth and Lerner reported that 'Approximately three times as many women as men have received psychosurgery.' The claim that psychosurgery has sometimes been used on women primarily to push women into traditional caring roles is supported by the overt statements of certain psycho-surgeons, one of whom observed that after a lobotomy 'some women do the dishes better, are better housewives and comply with the sexual demands of their husbands. . . . It takes away their aggressiveness.' (Roth and Lerner, 1974, p. 806.)

The doctor–patient relationship

Feminists do not simply object to the fact that many doctors hold very different views about women's role to those held by women themselves, and rarely hesitate to impose their own views on their patients. Feminists also complain that where female patients have attempted to challenge the dominant medical ideology of women's role both as patients and as mothers and wives, they have encountered very negative reactions from the medical profession. Doctors, or at least most doctors, appear to be particularly hostile to women's attempts to gain at least some control over medical decisions which may crucially affect their own physical and mental well-being. Some men may wish to object at this point that whilst feminist research has undoubtedly exposed some very negative aspects of doctors' behaviour towards female patients they have not proved that doctors actually treat women patients so differently from men. We would answer this objection in two ways. First we would suggest that if men believe that as a sex they are treated badly by the medical profession, it is up to them to produce substantive evidence to back up their hypothesis. Second we would point out that where direct comparisons have been made – and admittedly they are scarce – men appear to be treated less negatively than women by the medical profession. Research has shown, for example, that women patients are far more likely to be labelled as neurotic or over emotional by their doctors. Two British sociologists have made an interesting comparison of their treatment for migraine. Whereas David Oldman, a family man with a high powered job, never encountered any suggestion that his way of life was responsible for his attacks, Sally MacIntyre, as a single research student, was told that her migraine resulted from her not having a boyfriend and from her sublimation of her desire to have children. (MacIntyre and Oldman, 1977, p. 62.)

Doctors have certainly been accused of withholding medical information from patients of both sexes but a research study by Nio and Rosser suggests that British GPs are more likely to give vital information to male patients than to female patients. They found that when a group of GPs discussed how much information they would give to cancer patients, the examples of patients to whom they could give the diagnosis were mainly male whilst the examples of patients to whom they would not give the information were mainly female.

Female patients who attempt to have their views taken into consideration by their doctors often meet with very strong resistance. Sheila Kitzinger's study of pregnant women who had had their birth induced reports several women who were overtly or covertly threatened by their doctors into accepting induction. One patient was told, for example, 'If anything goes wrong, it will be your own fault.' A pregnant woman in a separate study who also tried to resist induction was told: 'I think you've got to assume if you come here for medical attention that we make all the decisions.' (Graham and Oakley, 1981, p. 63.)

Doctors themselves have openly argued that women, especially women needing some form of medical treatment, are by nature too emotional to play any useful role in medical decision making. Some British doctors use this argument, for example, to deny pregnant women any say in the decision of whether or not they should have an abortion.

Women who attempt to find out more about their own bodies rarely meet with professional approval. An NHS patient who simply asked some intelligent questions about her treatment had 'Watch this girl – she's a know-all' written in red across the top of her medical notes. (Bieggs, 1979, p. 9.)

As well as withholding information from them, doctors often seem very reluctant to accept that women patients may have any useful or reliable knowledge about themselves and their health problems. One hilarious example of this tendency is that of the doctor in an ante-natal clinic who would not at first accept that a mother knew the sex of her own children.

> Doctor (reading case notes): Ah, I see you've got a boy and a girl.
> Mother: No, two girls.
> Doctor: Really. Are you sure? I thought it said (checks in notes) Oh no, you're quite right, two girls. (Graham and Oakley, 1981, p. 66.)

In concluding this section we would claim that the (peculiarly) authoritarian stance taken by so many doctors towards female patients denies women any choice over a crucial aspect of their lives. Feminist critiques of medicine suggest that women are caught in a double bind. Either they play the submissive undemanding patient role expected of them, and run the risk of poor treatment, misdiagnosis and neglect or they try to make their own knowledge and views known to their doctor, in which case they run a severe risk of being labelled as demanding and therefore neurotic.

Social workers and women

Whilst all women will come into contact with a doctor at some point in their lives only a small minority of women will ever be social work clients. Moreover, the medical profession has undoubtedly exercised a much more powerful influence over the dominant ideology of women's role in our society than has the less prestigious and less firmly established profession of social work. Nevertheless, we would claim that social workers should be of particular interest to feminists on several grounds. First, both social workers and feminists are centrally concerned with the institution of the family and with women's role within it. Second, not only do women form the majority of social workers' clients, but even when they are not the direct 'problem' women are frequently targeted for social work intervention as the mothers, daughters or wives of those referred for social work help or supervision. According to Judy Hale:

> From within social work practice, just as from the traditional thriller, emerges the recurring theme of 'cherchez la femme'. The malfunctioning or dysfunctioning of families is seen as the

source of the majority of social work cases and in turn the woman of the family is viewed as the key person in maintaining the functioning of the family. It is not only her duty but her natural role to perform efficiently to this end. If the family has problems, therefore, and a social work case emerges, it is customary for workers to cast the woman in the role of villain of the piece. (Hale, 1983, p. 169.)

Third, social workers themselves, unlike doctors, are predominantly female although female social workers – like female doctors – have never exercised control over their profession nor over those organizations in which social work takes place.

The few writers who have begun to analyse social work from an explicitly feminist perspective have revealed that whilst the theoretical bases for the practice of social work may have changed radically over the last thirty years, they have yet to fully acknowledge and integrate the key feminist perspective that the personal is political and that the lives of women – as mothers, daughters and wives and as individuals in their own right – cannot be fully understood or changed without an understanding of the structural constraints and power relationships which determine women's collective and individual oppression within the family.

During the 1950s and 1960s psycho-dynamic theories and texts played a key role in social work training and development. A study of these texts reveals a clear sexist ideology of women's role and blatant gender stereotyping. Women were strictly defined in terms of their strong, unconscious urge towards motherhood, caring and femininity. Female clients who were distressed or depressed were diagnosed as having problems in adapting to their given feminine role. The alternative hypothesis – that the feminine role itself made some women unhappy or even sick – was nowhere entertained. As well as rigidly defining women's role, this psycho-dynamic literature also personalized women's problems. Student social workers of that time, many of whom are still practising today, were not taught that the problems faced by their individual female client's might have been more related to their position in society than to their individual psyches.

During the late 1960s and early 1970s a new radical approach to social work began to demolish some of the old psycho-dynamic theories about social workers' clients' problems. Marxist critiques of social work practice, particularly casework, put forward a class conflict model to explain the poor's problems and proposed collective struggle, political action and consciousness raising as radical alternatives to traditional social work activities. This radical literature, however, was not in any sense of the word feminist. Most of it was written by men who, when they did refer to women's role, related it to the demands of capitalism without discussing the equally relevant demands of patriarchy and of individual men (see for example Jones, 1975).

In the early 1980s many social work courses have begun to teach the methods of 'Family Therapy' although this type of therapy is still not widely used within local authority social services departments. Most Family Therapy textbooks are undoubtedly less overtly sexist than the older psycho-dynamic literature, but some feminists have accused Family Therapy of being intrinsically oppressive to women because of its tendency to accept uncritically the conventional nuclear family as the norm in our society. According to Bill Jordan, however, there is nothing intrinsically oppressive within the philosophy of Family Therapy because it does not actually have a philosophy. It is simply a range of therapeutic techniques or methods and as such is neither intrinsically repressive nor intrinsically liberating. Jordan does criticize Family Therapy, however, for failing to consider the key political and social contexts in which Family Therapy may take place. (Jordan, 1981.) Jordan's critique of Family Therapy is not explicitly feminist but it is relevant to a feminist analysis of social work methods and training. Family Therapy techniques may allow individual women to learn something about the dynamics of their own relationships within a particular family and they may even allow individual women to attempt to change those relationships, but as yet Family Therapy has failed to address the problem of women's collective oppression within a patriarchal/capitalist society and within the particular institution of the family which that society supports, and which in turn recreates women's oppression.

If social work literature is, in general, still uninformed and uninforming about gender issues in social work, what evidence do we have about social work practice? Unfortunately, not a great deal, but the snippets of information and analysis which feminists have produced suggest that many social workers still hold traditional attitudes about women's natural and proper functions within the family and in society in general. The small amount of evidence we have also suggests that professional social workers may play a similar role to doctors in controlling, or at least attempting to control, their female clients' lives, in ways which feminists regard as sexist and oppressive.

Social workers, women and sexuality

Annie Hudson's analysis of social workers' reactions to 'deviant' adolescent girls suggests that many social workers continue to define women as deviant if they do not follow the traditional female path towards marriage and motherhood. According to Hudson social workers tend to define adolescent girls as being 'at risk' if they are seen to be in danger of becoming promiscuous and/or pregnant. Hudson accepts that girls who spend their time on the streets with 'the wrong sort of men' may be in genuine danger, but she challenges the conventional social work wisdom that these girls are at risk from themselves and therefore in need of treatment to cure them of their deviant behaviour. 'What needs to be contested', she suggests, 'is whether they are at risk from themselves (as may be implied by reception into care), or whether the dangers lie in the potential of male violence and exploitation on the street.' (Hudson, 1983, p. 11.) Hudson claims that social workers' treatment of 'wayward' adolescent girls is frequently a type of social control. Both capitalism and patriarchy, she suggests, are threatened when girls reject passive femininity and openly express their sexuality or exhibit aggressive tendencies. Girls who stray too far from the traditional paths towards marriage and motherhood become the focus for concern and social work 'supervision'. They are then defined as not 'fully feminine' and as suitable cases for treatment. They may also evoke social workers' deep seated and perhaps even unconscious fears about the uncontrollably sexual female. Hudson quotes one social worker in her study describing an adolescent under her care thus: 'J is a very promiscuous girl, if all that she tells the other girls is true, then no young man is safe.' (Hudson, 1984.)

As well as exposing the sexist assumptions underlying social workers' reactions to aggressive or particularly sexually active adolescent girls, feminists have also analysed social workers' reactions to the sexual abuse of young girls within their own families. According to Elizabeth Wilson social workers and other welfare professionals still tend to ignore evidence of incest mainly because they just 'do not want to see anything' which threatens their view of what family life ought to be like. Wilson admits that social workers face many practical difficulties when dealing with incest and that they may be right to be reluctant to take children away from their families too readily, but she criticizes social workers for accepting certain myths about incest, particularly the myth of 'mother collusion'. Mothers of sexually abused children are frequently labelled sexually frigid or castrating and then blamed for colluding in their husband's abuse of their children. (Wilson, 1983.) Annie Hudson argues that by failing to place the blame for incest firmly on the male abuser, social workers avoid facing up to the feminist insight that the family is not a private haven for women but is all too often an unsafe prison. She concludes:

> Social workers are prepared to take an active role in protecting young women from the dangers of prostitution and becoming pregnant, but not from the abuse and violence of their fathers. This is a reflection of the myth that women are unsafe on the street but not in the home where they receive the supposed protection of their male guardians. (Hudson, 1984.)

Social workers and women's caring role

According to Barrett and McIntosh the nuclear family oppresses the majority of women not because they face violence or sexual abuse within it but because they face the daily grind of isolated drudgery: 'The daily regime in the prison is not the drama of violence or rape: it is the long hours of working banged up in a solitary cell while the guards attend to other, more important business.' (Barrett and McIntosh, 1982, p. 58.)

Yet social workers still tend to blame those women who fail to cope adequately with this role. Judy Hale quotes from several case files which illustrate this tendency. One stated, for example,

> Inadequate manipulative woman whose tendency to depression leads her to neglect her home and family. In spite of a supportive husband she does not seem able to function in her role as wife and mother, although there has been no success in persuading her not to have more children. (Hale, 1983, p. 171.)

If practising social workers still tend to see depressed women as failing to perform their natural role in the family rather than as being depressed by that very role they also sometimes fail to give adequate help to those women who decide to escape from an intolerable family situation. A quarter of battered women in a national survey of women in refuges complained that social workers had either tried to reconcile them to their violent partners or had tried to stop them leaving. One woman commented: 'I rang social services because I was so desperate to leave and they said, "all we can do if you leave is we'll take the children off you and take them into care and we don't want that do we?" So I said "no" and that was it.' (Binney, Harkell and Nixon, 1981, p. 19.) In 1977 a random survey of 103 case records written by social workers in a northern town revealed that over a third of cases involved domestic violence, frequently very severe but in only three cases were the social workers primarily concerned about the violence against women. Their main concern in the great majority of these cases was for the children. Several social workers had discussed the problem of violence with the woman concerned but only very rarely had the violent man himself been contacted.

Even the most radical feminist would no doubt accept that it is not unreasonable for social workers to be primarily concerned about the effects of violence within the family on children. Feminists may also understand why male-dominated social work and medical institutions have failed to focus attention on the problem of violent men holding positions of power within the nuclear family. They cannot, however, condone the effects of this failure on women.

Social workers not only continue to expect women to be good wives and mothers within the patriarchal institutions of the family, they also tend to reinforce women's role as unpaid carers of the elderly and the disabled and certain social workers still appear to believe that women are natural carers and that they have a duty to care.

One study of gender differences in an old people's home found that the residential staff displayed overt hostility towards frail elderly women who had been admitted with their husbands. Despite the extreme frailty of these women the staff appeared to blame them for not continuing to provide normal caring services for their husbands. Judith Oliver's study of the lack of state support for wives caring for severely disabled husbands also illustrates social workers' readiness to assume that women can care without any outside help. (Oliver, 1983.)

The tradition within social work of identifying one member of a family as 'the client' may lead social workers to identify with the needs of the cared for rather than the carer, and thus to ignore the problems faced by many female care-givers. An illustration of this – possibly inadvertent – bias is the current interest in 'granny battering'. As Traynor and Hasnip have pointed out, most research into this emotive subject has focused on the plight of the cared for, yet a study of caring relatives by Suzanne Steinmetz found that while 3 per cent of care-givers 'hit or slapped' their elderly dependants, 22 per cent of these dependants 'hit, slapped or threw objects at' their care-giving children. So where are the headlines about battered care-givers? (Traynor and Hasnip, 1984.)

A social worker reading this section might well protest that as a profession social workers do not have the power to procure enough material resources for their deprived and oppressed female clients. They are therefore forced to push women into the role of unpaid carers and to attempt to make individual women more effective carers rather than providing them with any alternative caring services or resources. We accept the logic of this defence of social work but we nevertheless claim that individual casework with deprived families is often a form of social control over individual women rather than a means of support for them. Whilst radical critics of professional social workers have been forcibly arguing for some time that casework is too often a type of social control they have not pointed out that it is predominantly women who are the targets of this control. It is most often mothers whose parenting is subjected to the closest scrutiny once their children have been placed on an 'at risk' register. It is mothers who are advised how to manage their resources and budget more efficiently regardless of whether or not the income they receive from their husbands or from the State is sufficient to meet all the family's basic needs. Perhaps because – at least until recently – fathers tended to be out at work when social workers visited, one very rarely hears of social workers working with fathers to improve their financial skills!

Since 1972 feminism has made an impact on social work training and more feminist social workers are going into practice. But the world which they are entering is actually more oppressive than it was in the early 1970s. More children from deprived families are being taken into care compulsorily, fewer resources are available to provide supportive services for the caring female relatives of the severely disabled and handicapped and central government is pursuing an ideological and an economic campaign to push women even more firmly into the home. Despite a limited rise of feminism within the social work profession there is little evidence that social work practitioners are successfully fighting these repressive trends and some evidence, for example in the hard line approach to taking 'at risk' children into care more readily, that some social workers are actively participating in the implementation of new social policies which emphasize tighter controls over women's roles as wives, mothers and carers rather than the more caring aspects of the welfare services.

Conclusion

In this chapter we have presented an almost wholly negative, feminist account of the relationship between welfare professionals and their female clients. We must emphasize, however, that welfare professionals do not invariably oppress female clients. Indeed, in a number of ways the existence of relatively powerful and autonomous welfare professions acts as an important and beneficial buffer between women and the patriarchal/capitalist state. For example, despite strong and concerted attempts by certain pressure groups and politicians in recent years to further restrict women's access to contraception and abortion services, the medical profession has strongly and effectively resisted all such restrictions. Consultants have continued to carry out 'social' abortions despite considerable pressure from the DHSS itself. Certain doctors have put their own careers at risk by carrying out 'late' abortions despite a campaign to prosecute them for doing so. Finally, despite a strong media campaign led by Mrs Victoria Gillick, which has had a preliminary victory, doctors, with backing from the BMA, are still fighting for the right to prescribe 'the pill' to girls under the age of sixteen without informing their parents.

It is more difficult to provide specific examples where either the teaching profession or the social work profession has defended women against oppressive campaigns or social policy initiatives. But, we can at least suggest that the traditional autonomy of the teaching profession over the school curriculum has played some part in deterring the present Conservative Government from implementing its plans to reinforce traditional family roles through the school curriculum. Social workers, nurses and other welfare providers have also fought against cuts in welfare services which leave even more caring to be done by unpaid female relatives. Unfortunately we simply cannot measure the extent to which individual feminist or pro-feminist teachers and social workers have attempted – perhaps not always successfully – to work in ways which support rather than control their female pupils or clients.

Despite the fact that women may have benefited in some ways from the powers which the State has given to professional welfare providers, we believe there is an essential paradox contained in the relationship between welfare professionals and their female clients. Whilst professional power enables some welfare providers to protect women from certain oppressive moves by the State or powerful interest groups, this same power ultimately oppresses female welfare clients by perpetuating their powerlessness and lack of autonomy over key aspects of their lives. Let us explore this paradox a little more fully.

One of the key characteristics or skills which professionals are deemed to possess is their ability to define welfare needs. It is because both politicians and society in general believe that professionals have the special skills required to define and meet certain types of welfare needs that professionals are allowed so much freedom and control over their own services. Equally, if not more importantly, welfare professionals themselves are socialized into believing that they do indeed have special skills and that as professionals they must defend this right to define their clients' needs against anyone who challenges it. This basic tenet of professionalism means that professionals will strongly resist any attempts by the State to interfere with or restrict their autonomous definitions of welfare needs. Sometimes – particularly perhaps when central government is imbued with a right-wing ideology – professionals' brave defence of their own autonomy will benefit their female clients. It is not difficult, however, to imagine a rather different set of circumstances in which professionals' defence of their own power against encroachments by the State would not be in the best interests of welfare clients. Ironically the Conservative Government's recent attempt to cut welfare expenditure by restricting doctors' freedom to prescribe brand name tranquillizers which was strongly resisted by the medical profession may actually be of benefit to some women who are at present targets for profit-seeking drugs companies. A government which planned to introduce NHS abortions on demand might also be resisted by a significant majority of the medical profession on the grounds that they alone have the special expertise to judge whether or not an abortion will be in particular patients' long-term interests. In other words, doctors would, and do, claim that they are better able to define their patients' needs than either the State or patients themselves. It is this conviction, held by most, if not all, welfare professionals, that ultimately oppresses women as welfare clients. Feminists believe that until women themselves exert real power over their own sexuality and reproductive functions they cannot be free in other areas of their lives. Feminists also claim that women must break out of their subordinate family role in order to gain equality in the work place. They can only achieve this liberation from the unpaid caring duties of wife, mother and daughter if they can break away from the dominant ideology of women's caring role and gain control over the material resources needed to provide alternatives to unpaid caring individual women. One of the barriers between women and these keys to liberation is welfare professionalism.

Of course, we are fully aware that the shortage of resources such as home helps and free day care for the under fives is beyond professionals' control and, we acknowledge that many welfare professionals have fought very hard – if unsuccessfully – to protect and even increase these scarce resources. Nevertheless, whilst acknowledging the many restraints imposed on professionals by the State and by the statutory institutions in which they work, we would still claim that by acting as the rationers of scarce resources welfare professionals provide a useful buffer between women's demands and a State which will not meet those demands. Welfare professionals, rationing resources on a personal and individual basis, help to disguise the collective nature of women's oppression. They keep individual female clients in a competitive submissive position. In order to get what they want from the State individual female welfare clients have to please their own doctor, social worker or teacher. They have virtually no power as individual supplicants to get what they want by fighting the system.

Even welfare professionals who are sympathetic to feminist demands cannot, by the very nature of their position, fully support the most radical demands for women themselves to have complete control over a range of welfare resources. As professionals working within professionally dominated institutions, they cannot totally escape either the ideology of professionalism which gives them sole right to define patients' needs, or the material and legal reality of their power over the clients who turn to them for help. They cannot, therefore, give to their female clients full autonomy and equality within the traditional welfare provider/welfare consumer relationship.

6

The material impact of welfare

In the previous chapter we looked at the way in which welfare professionals play a role in the socialization of women, and reinforce gender stereotypes which restrict women's ability to define their own needs and interests. In this chapter we shall move away from these less tangible forms of coercion to look at the way similar ideologies have come to be embodied in social policies providing material support for women and men. In particular, we shall examine the way in which cash benefits for the economically dependent, practical care for the physically dependent, and housing provision, embody assumptions about the family and women's role: in particular that the nuclear family is the norm, that married and cohabiting women are supported financially by a male breadwinner, and that they are available to act as unpaid carers of those who are physically dependent.

We shall begin by demonstrating that these assumptions exist. In this, we can point to a growing body of feminist research. We shall then consider the relationships between the assumptions about women's role, their actual role, and the material impact of welfare. It is all too easy to uncover crass sexism in legislation, and to repeat the inanities of politicians. Equally, perhaps more important, is the need to show how in *practice* such policies shape women's lives. In following this approach, we discover that social policy is in fact extremely contradictory, in part because the interests of men as a sex, men as capitalists and men as state functionaries intersect and sometimes conflict in quite complicated ways.

Social security and women's dependency

The two main ways in which the social security system embodies
assumptions about women's economic dependency are, first, the
limitations on a married or cohabiting woman's right to claim
benefit in her own right and, second, the exclusion of married
women from certain benefits on the grounds that unpaid
housework is their normal 'job'.

The British system of social security is divided into two distinct
systems: the insurance system which is based on benefits provided
as of right if past contributions have been paid, and a system of
assistance, financed out of general taxation. We saw in chapter 1
how the insurance systems had difficulty in coming to terms with
the fact that married women were part of the labour market. The
1946 National Insurance Act perpetuated the system whereby all
insured married women workers paid lower contributions to the
scheme in return for lower benefits. In addition, Beveridge's
assumption that they would, more often than not, be engaged in
'more important' unpaid work at home was translated into the
'married woman's option', whereby married women workers
could opt out of all insurance contributions apart from those
attributable to the industrial injuries scheme. Contemporary
feminist critics of the Beveridge Report argued that the married
woman's option legitimated married women's secondary position
in the labour market. Abbott and Bompas (1943) for example
argued that Beveridge's recommendations created 'a class of pin
money worker' (p. 10). This feminist perspective had little
resonance to the extent that a major textbook on social security
published in 1967 argued that the married woman's option
represented 'preferential treatment to married women' (George,
1968, p. 20).

The original national insurance scheme involved flat rate
contributions and benefits. With the introduction of graduated,
and later earnings-related contributions and benefits from 1959,
women included in the scheme were treated the same as men.
Thus an anomalous position was created whereby for some
benefits married women were classed separately, whereas for
others no distinctions were drawn as to marital status. This
situation is now being remedied by the provision in the 1975
Social Security Benefits Act, for the phasing out of the married
woman's option from 1977. The 1978 EEC Directive on Equal
Treatment for Men and Women in Social Security is also leading
to many other discriminatory aspects of the national insurance
system being removed. Under the 1980 Social Security Act, for

example, women claiming unemployment and sickness benefit are able to claim the additional allowances for children which have previously only been available to male claimants. A wife is also able to claim for her husband where he earns less than the allowance.

The more glaring instances of the social security system assuming women's dependency are now within the social assistance system, where the notion of rights in relation to contribution is absent. The main assistance measure is Supplementary Benefit which provides a means tested income for those not in work who have either too few or no insurance contributions, or whose needs are estimated as being above the level of their insurance benefit. Until recently, married or cohabiting women could not claim benefit at all – if they lived with a man who was working, they were assumed to be supported by him, regardless of whether in fact this occurred. If both partners were unemployed, the regulations stated that: 'Where a husband and wife are members of the same household their requirements and resources shall be aggregated and shall be treated as the husband's.' (1976 Supplementary Benefits Act.)

Politicians showed themselves extremely reluctant to change the situation. O'Malley, Minister of State at the DHSS in a letter to a group campaigning for changes in the system argued:

It is normal for a married woman in this country to be primarily supported by her husband, and she looks to him for support when not actually working, rather than to social security benefit. ... The number of instances of the wife having chosen to be the breadwinner, as opposed to having taken on that role, is still very small. Indeed, it continues to be a widespread view that a husband who is capable of work has a duty to society, as well as to his wife, to provide the primary support for his family.
(Quoted in London Women's Liberation Campaign for Legal and Financial Independence and Rights of Women, 1979, p. 20.)

This statement shows the blend of normative and empirical arguments: women *aren't* breadwinners, but this is 'normal'; women 'don't' look to social security, but the system is formed in such a way as to reinforce and legitimate their dependence.

The cohabitation rule has come under attack from a number of directions. Pressure groups on behalf of the poor such as Child Poverty Action Group (CPAG) emphasize the hardship and indignity caused to women who end up being supported by neither the State nor the men they live with (or whom officials *claim* they live with). The Supplementary Benefit regulations refer rather coyly to 'living together as man and wife' – a vague concept, but one which has led to allegations that the special investigators responsible for administering the rule are 'sex snoopers'. However sensitive an investigator, the intrusion into the privacy of women's personal lives is an embarrassing and humiliating experience (see, for example, Lister, 1973).

The now defunct Claimants Union, an organization *of* rather than on behalf of those dependent on social security, also made opposition to the cohabitation rule one of its central campaigns during the early 1970s. The main difference between the Claimants Union and the CPAG was in its grass roots/direct action approach to campaigning, rather than its programme for reform of the Supplementary Benefit system.

Feminists' distinctive contribution has been to link the issue of hardship and bureaucratic insensitivity to the wider principle that women should be treated as independent individuals throughout the income maintenance and taxation systems. Feminists have called for disaggregation of needs and benefits such that any man or woman can claim benefits in their own right and be treated separately for the purposes of taxation. Such an approach may coincide with the demands of the 'poverty lobby', for example, both oppose the cohabitation rule. On the other hand, CPAG has attempted to gain legitimacy for its policies by emphasizing the needs of *children*, and more recently under the directorship of Frank Field, the interests of *families* (see, for example, Field, 1980). In these respects, the poverty lobby has worked within the framework of the dominant ideology of the family which feminists believe must be challenged.

The feminist approach has been consistently rejected by the DHSS, although in 1978 its review of the Supplementary Benefit system suggested that it might be possible to introduce more flexibility into the system such that either the man or the woman in a household could be nominated as breadwinner (DHSS, 1978). Once again, the EEC Directive has led to action, and from November 1983 it has been possible for a woman to be nominated breadwinner where she has been in work during the previous six months. Whilst this may be seen as a degree of equal treatment, it continues to treat the family as the unit for assessment, and thus comes nowhere near meeting the feminist demand for disaggregation.

Benefits relating to disability were ruled as being outside the ambit of the EEC Directive, and blatant discrimination against married women continues to operate. Invalid Care Allowance, for example, is available to men and single women who have to care full-time for a severely disabled relative. Married and cohabiting women are excluded. Similar discrimination exists in relation to Non-Contributory Invalidity Pension. Men and single women simply have to demonstrate that they are unfit for paid work in order to qualify. Married or cohabiting women, however, have to demonstrate that they cannot perform 'usual household duties', involving tests as to whether they can make beds and clean the kitchen floor. Nothing could illustrate more clearly the view that women's normal 'job' is housework. The test causes much confusion and resentment. In the words of one disabled woman: 'It is bad enough to suffer physically but to suffer the degradation of a type of physical means test is beyond belief.' (EOC, 1981b, p. 9.)

After a review of the scheme (DHSS, 1983), the Minister for the Disabled announced in December 1983 that the Government planned to abolish the household duties test and replace it with a common medical test for all claimants. Since this test will be more stringent, it will exclude some men and women who qualify under the current rules. The additional cost of this equal treatment is estimated to be £20 million. In 1982, however, it was estimated that the cost of simply abolishing the household duties test and using the current medical test would be £100 million. This illustrates a more general point. We have reached the stage where governments tend not to oppose equal treatment for men and women on principle, but are only willing to concede it in practice if the cost can be kept to a minimum. Equal treatment means worse treatment for all. This is perhaps most blatant in relation to short term national insurance benefits. We saw above how the Government has reshaped the insurance scheme so as to enable women to claim the additional allowances for dependants. At the same time, however, it has phased out the dependent child additions from all short term benefits. What one hand gives, the other takes away.

Women and the care of dependants

The income maintenance system assumes that married women are supported by their husbands, and their normal role is that of housewife. Similarly, services in kind to support the dependent population of elderly, disabled and children assume that married women are available to take on this role, and that state services are there to supplement their activities and fill gaps only in the absence of female relatives.

As regards children, the ideology that mothers should be full-time carers and that children are emotionally and physically healthier if their mothers do not work outside the home, has strong support and is reflected in the division between nursery *education* and nursery *care*. Nursery education has been encouraged, particularly since the Plowden Report in 1967, as part of a strategy for combating educational deprivation. As such, nursery education is looked upon favourably by politicians who are totally opposed to day care for children to enable mothers to work outside the home. Nursery schools/classes are of little help to working mothers because they operate during school hours and terms, and many children attend only part-time. The numbers of children receiving some nursery education is very high – in several inner city authorities more than half of three- and four-year-olds attend classes.

Day care, on the other hand, is run by the Social Services rather than Education Departments, reflecting a concern about social need/social problems rather than either education, or a mother's right to work. Official day care is provided in local authority and voluntary day nurseries and by registered child minders; unofficial care, by unregistered minders. In practice, places in day nurseries are so scarce that they are usually limited to children from single parent families or where social workers fear potential or actual child abuse. In 1976, for example, there were 16.3 places for children in all kinds of official day care nurseries per 1,000 children under the age of five. The task of caring for the children of working parents thus falls to the registered and unregistered child minders. In other words, the State takes virtually no responsibility for this aspect of care.

This was not always the case. During the Second World War the State desperately needed all the workers it could get, even married female ones. It, therefore, began to encourage mothers to work full-time with a number of incentives including the rapid expansion of free state nurseries. In July 1941 there were only thirty-six full-time state nurseries. By 1944 there were 1,431. As soon as the war ended and soldiers returned from the front expecting jobs, the official line was that mothers should once more be expected and encouraged to stay at home both for their own good and for the good of their children. In 1945 a Ministry of Health Circular stated:

The Ministers concerned accept the view of medical and other authorities that, in the interests of health and development of the child no less than for the benefit of the mother, the proper place for a child under two is at home with the mother. They are also of the opinion that, under normal peacetime conditions, the right policy to pursue would be positively to discourage mothers of children under two from going out to work. . . .   (Quoted in Wilson, 1977, p. 154.)

The run-down of the war-time system of day-nurseries cannot be attributed solely to ideological beliefs about the mother–child relationship and women's role. Ann Dally points out that whilst psychological theories such as those of John Bowlby were important, they might not have proved so popular with policy makers if they had not supported a line which was cheap and convenient. It was expensive for the government to run nurseries which had been set up to encourage mothers to work during the war 'so there were strong political pressures to save money and reduce unemployment by pushing women back into the home and finding moral justification for doing so.' (Dally, 1982, p. 96.)

Today, the truncated day nursery provision of the post-war Welfare State is being cut further. Contemporary Conservatives do not need to invoke any new childcare 'expert' such as Bowlby to justify their policies: a call for a return to traditional family values and responsibilities is seen as appealing in itself, and is an important aspect of the New Right's attempt to roll back the frontiers of the state. Privatization of childcare by making women responsible for young children, complements other aspects of the Conservatives' privatization strategy towards the Welfare State through the sale of assets such as housing and the contracting out of service provision to private companies. Present day childcare policy is about ideology: but it is an ideology about the role of the family in relation to the state rather than the mother–child relationship.

The motive of keeping down public expenditure is rather more marked when it comes to looking at provision for the frail elderly. A recent report estimated the annual value of care provided by families at £3.7 to 5.3 *billions* compared with £928 millions spent on personal social services for the over seventy-fives (Family Policy Studies Centre, 1984). Despite the attention that residential care has received, only a tiny fraction of the elderly are institutionalized. For the vast majority, the alternative state policy is 'community care', which as feminists have been quick to point out, means family care which usually means care by women (Finch and Groves, 1980). Hunt (1978) estimated that in 1976 there were some two million women caring for dependent adult relatives, and a small scale survey in North Tyneside during 1979–80 found that there were more people caring for adult relatives than there were mothers of children under sixteen (Briggs, undated). Many carers are responsible for more than one adult – 54 per cent of members of the Association of Carers are in this position (Oliver, 1982). All surveys show the vast majority of carers to be female and that female carers receive less help than their male counterparts (Walker, 1983 provides a useful summary of research).

Although domiciliary services such as home helps, district nursing and laundry services are provided by statutory authorities, in practice carers receive little or no support, and scarce services tend to be channelled to the frail elderly who live alone. An EOC survey of 111 households containing an elderly or handicapped dependant found that only 14 per cent received a free home help, and only 9 per cent made use of a day centre (EOC, 1980).

If housework on its own can be exhausting caring for severely dependent relatives can be even more physically demanding and emotionally draining. Feminists have now gathered an impressive amount of empirical evidence which reveals the physical, emotional and financial costs borne by those women who care for severely dependent relatives. According to an EOC report on 'the experience of caring for elderly and handicapped dependants' many of the carers interviewed spoke of health problems which they felt had been caused or seriously aggravated by their caring responsibilities. Bad backs were the most common complaint brought on by heavy lifting – but the report noted 'Bad back or not, the responsibility remains theirs.' Carers' mental health also suffered. 'Quite a number said they suffered from constant depression whilst others spoke of "nerves", "tension" and "stress". One woman concluded desperately "I think that before long I shall be in a mental home."' (EOC, 1980, p. 29.)

Not surprisingly, therefore, feminists have argued that 'the community' is: 'an ideological portmanteau word for reactionary, conservative ideology that oppresses women by silently confining them to the private sphere without as much as even mentioning them.' (Wilson, 1982, p. 55.)

Community care is by no means exclusively a right-wing anti-collectivist solution to the needs of the frail elderly. Certain sections of the left have also embraced the concept of community care, not as a cheap option nor as a ploy for reducing the role of the Welfare State but as possibly the best overall solution to meeting the needs of those families who clearly *want* to care and those elderly people who 'obviously' prefer to be cared for by their own families (for example, Harris, 1985). Despite the very wide gap between a left-wing version of community care for the elderly and the more dominant right-wing version, feminists have suggested that those on the left share with the right certain fundamental assumptions about women's caring role. They assume, for example, that personal loving care by female relatives within the family is more or less universally preferable to both carers and cared for than 'impersonal' 'institutional' forms of caring. Institutional care is therefore usually regarded as a second best option or back up option to be used as a last resort when families either do not exist or fail to provide the loving care which is their normal freely undertaken duty. Although some left-wing proponents of community care acknowledge that men may sometimes wish to care for their dependent relatives and that the State might even attempt to facilitate this 'non-sexist' option, their proposals for left-wing versions of community care rarely challenge the view that women are 'natural' carers. Indeed many 'good' experimental schemes designed to provide 'real' community – as opposed to family – care for the elderly have relied heavily on women volunteers or on women as very low paid workers. A report from the Kent Community Care Scheme, for example, stated that people offering help ranged from 'those with previous caring experiences, such as retired nurses, to young housewives with time to spare'. To which Janet Finch has added 'Not too many men it seems.' Finch's review of such schemes concluded 'the "caring" envisaged in these alternative community care schemes will remain women's work for the foreseeable future for both economic and ideological reasons' (Finch, 1984, p. 11).

Housing – the most fundamental need

Compared with income maintenance, childcare and community care policies, housing has received relatively little attention from feminists. Yet housing provision is fundamental to the achievement of the feminist goal of giving women choices other than the norm of the bourgeois family. As Watson and Austerberry point out: 'Both access to housing, and the quality of housing available structure not only the divisions between rich and poor, but also sexual divisions between men and women.' (Watson and Austerberry, 1980, p. 61.)

The British housing system is extremely unequal: both in terms of the physical condition of individual houses, the quality of housing location, and the economic costs and benefits, and social status of different tenure groups. A wealth of literature has been produced by Fabian and Marxist critics of this system showing how it not only reflects, but also reinforces inequalities between rich and poor. Only recently however, have feminists such as Watson and Austerberry begun to argue that housing inequality also reproduces gender inequality.

Lone women tend to be vulnerable in the housing market because of their relatively low earning power which is further reduced if they have had children and been economically dependent on their partner. Women can find themselves without a partner in a variety of circumstances: they may have chosen to remain single and childless; they may be unmarried mothers; or their marriage may have broken down. In the first case, the well-paid professional single woman is in a position little different from that of her male colleague, particularly since the 1975 Sex Discrimination Act outlawed discrimination against women in the granting of tenancies and mortgages. Similarly, two childless working women living together will probably find it difficult to gain a local authority tenancy, but as a two-income household, will probably be able to afford a private sector solution to their housing needs.

The majority of women, however, are not in well-paid jobs when single, and will go on to marry and have children thus further reducing their earning capacity. If their relationship breaks down their economic vulnerability is compounded by the operation of the housing system. The way this occurs is crucially affected by whether or not a woman is responsible for dependent children. If she is, she may not find access to housing such a major problem as other women, but she will be penalized by being channelled into poor quality, local authority housing.

The 1981 Census showed that 57 per cent of single parent households were council tenants compared with 25 per cent of households headed by a married man. Only 31 per cent of single parent households were owner occupiers, compared with 72 per cent of families consisting of a married couple with two children. Single parents are also penalized within the local authority sector by receiving worse accommodation in terms of condition and location. (See Murie, 1983 for a useful summary of evidence on housing conditions.)

The reasons for this are complex. Direct discrimination due to hostile attitudes on the part of housing allocators may be part of the explanation. Many authorities have been slow to adopt allocation procedures based solely on housing need, and have continued to use systems which allow personal prejudice to influence decisions. However, bias may creep in even where none is exercised against single parents as such. If the system discriminates against categories of applicants which include large numbers of single parents, they will inevitably suffer. This type of indirect discrimination has been noted in relation to race but less attention has been paid to gender. However, indirect discrimination may arise because single parents are particularly vulnerable to homelessness, and homeless families are treated less favourably than those rehoused through the waiting list – for example by the authority making only one offer of accommodation. Whether a woman is an unmarried mother living with her parents, or a married woman, she is vulnerable to the breakdown of relationships on which her right to housing depends. Such relationship breakdown will tend to lead to homelessness. Nationally, just over a third of families accepted as homeless are single parents. Recent research in Manchester, however, shows that a staggering 70 per cent of homeless families in the city are single parent families.

A third of women admitted to temporary accommodation in Manchester were homeless because of marital disputes or violence. Despite changes in the law which have improved women's legal rights to exclude violent men from their home, even when the tenancy, or ownership is in the man's name, women's physical vulnerability in the face of male violence leads them to choose homelessness rather than exercise formal legal rights.

We referred above to the fact that women with dependent children are best placed as regards access to housing. This is largely the result of the 1977 Housing (Homeless) Persons Act which gave local authorities a duty to house homeless people in 'priority need', a category which includes all women with children who have no home, or cannot return because of the threat of domestic violence. We would not, however, like to suggest that the Act has solved the problem of access to housing for women with children. The National Women's Aid Federation which brings together the local Women's Aid Groups running refuges for battered women, has documented the wide variation in local authority practice regarding rehousing of battered women. Many continue to use arguments such as that a woman made herself 'intentionally homeless' to deny rehousing (NWAF, 1978).

Women without dependent children can find themselves with

few options in the housing market. Particularly hard hit are women who have been carers – either of children or dependent adult relatives – but who are now alone. We saw in the previous section how many women have given up their paid jobs to become carers, and for some this has been a lifetime's work as they have cared first for their children and then their ageing parents. For married women, divorce may leave them without a home in middle age, with little prospect of earning a livelihood or finding decent housing. Austerberry and Watson quote the case of a middle-aged army wife, who had spent twenty-three years in Kenya before her marriage broke up:

> 'I got the boot. I was packed on the aeroplane and sent home – England was still "home" for me'. She arrived back with no job and nowhere to go. She stayed for three months with her daughter, where there was little room, and then moved out to a hostel where she has lived for three years.
>
> (Austerberry and Watson, 1983, p. 9)

A woman married to a man who owns their home is in a slightly better position. Since the 1967 Matrimonial Homes Act, she is entitled to a share of the property, usually fixed by judges at a half of its value. After the mortgage has been repaid, such a sum will not usually enable a woman to buy a house of her own if her earning prospects are poor. A similar situation may arise when single women continue to live in their parents' home. When the parents die, if the property is part of the inheritance of several children, the single woman may find herself homeless.

None of these women are classed as in 'priority need' under the 1977 Act, unless they are vulnerable due to old age or physical/mental infirmity. The problem of homeless women on their own has tended to receive little attention – it is seen as less of a problem than that of men because there are fewer women in hostels compared with men. However, Austerberry and Watson argue that the fact that there is less *provision* does not mean that there is less *need*. Homeless women on their own are still a concealed group within the housing system.

Apart from access to housing, house design is also very important in structuring people's lives. We saw in chapter 1 how women during the inter-war years became involved with minor issues to do with house design – they were called in to advise on the nitty gritties of the siting of sinks and cookers from the 'point of view of the housewife'. A feminist approach to design starts from the proposition that there *are* no housewives, or as an intermediate step, that necessary, individual housework should be reduced to the minimum. This requires a radical re-appraisal of the single family, suburban housing which has come to represent an ideal for many men and women. As Friedan argues:

> That suburban dream house literally embodied in brick or wood or concrete block, as it sat on its 60-by-100 . . . lot, the feminine mystique, and trapped women in it . . . That isolated house, with all those appliances each woman had to spend all day operating by herself, somehow made us spend more time doing housework than our mothers and grandmothers . . .
>
> (Friedan, 1983, p. 282)

There have always been radicals in architecture who have put forward alternatives such as convenient flats including communal facilities such as laundries. The record of such experiments in Britain – for example the Quarry Hill estate in Leeds – is not inspiring (see for example, Ravetz 1974). Nevertheless, there has never been an attempt to place women's ideas and women's needs at the centre of such planning, and to make the funds available to ensure that they work. For such a vision, Friedan turns to the Swedish concept of 'service housing' which has proved popular:

> People had their own apartments, pleasant living rooms, bedrooms, balcony terrace, and small kitchenettes, but they also had a common child-care center, a nursery for babies, and an after school programme. There was a common kitchen and dining room where all could take their meals – or pick them up after work to eat in their own apartments.
>
> (Friedan, 1983, p. 216)

If there is a lesson from such successes and failures, it is that housing is too important to be left to the fragmented expertise of professionals – the design, financing and running of housing schemes must be integrated and must take account of women's needs and interests.

Conclusion – The contradictions of social policy

The assumptions underlying social security and social care policies are, as we have seen, that women are economically dependent on their husbands and that they are therefore available to act as unpaid carers for the dependent population of children, elderly and disabled people. It all fits together very neatly – and of course if couples always remained married, if husbands never became unemployed, employers hadn't had the crafty idea of increasing profits through employing women workers, and women were content to perform unpaid labours of love, there would be few problems. But of course life isn't perfect! In this section we shall explore some contradictions between the assumption in social policy of women's dependency, and economic and social reality.

This contradiction operates at a number of levels. In the first place the rising incidence of divorce, currently running at one in three of first marriages has led to a considerable increase in the number of single parent families, most of whom are headed by women. In 1974, the Finer Committee estimated that there were 620,000 one parent families containing 1.08 million children. Today estimates of the number of single parents vary from around 800,000 to a million (Rossiter, 1983). Even more women and children experience lone parenthood at some stage in their lives.

The income maintenance system has attempted to walk a tightrope between maintaining the idea that lone mothers and their children are supported by their former partners, and acknowledging the reality that most are wholly, or largely unsupported. Thus, for example, the supplementary benefits system has had to acknowledge the fact that many former husbands do not pay maintenance, and pay lone parents their full needs allowance rather than deducting from it the mother's maintenance award.

The contradiction between rising divorce and the idea that men should support their wives and children has also been highlighted by pressure groups representing former husbands and their second wives, who have popularized the stereotype of the former wife as 'alimony drone'. Dick Allen of the Campaign for Justice in Divorce argued on Radio 4's 'You the Jury': 'current divorce law allows a woman to divorce her husband but remain married to his purse.' (Quoted in Brophy, 1984, p. 115.)

Despite the evidence that few women without dependent children receive maintenance, and that in the typical situation: 'payments were often at a low level, infrequently uprated and not regularly paid' (Popay *et al.* 1983, p. 43), the mud sticks. The 1984 Matrimonial and Family Proceedings Act has introduced changes in the law which may limit the amount and duration of former wives' maintenance.

A second aspect of the contradiction between ideology of the economically dependent wife/mother and material reality arises because neither the 'family wage' earned by husbands in employment nor state child benefit are adequate to support a family with children. Family Allowances for all but the first child were introduced in 1945 at a level of 5/- (25p) a week, at which level they remained until the 1950s. Since then, they have of course been uprated, but their real value has fluctuated considerably. As a percentage of average earnings, child endowment for two children was at its peak at around 10 per cent in 1955–6 and 1965–6. In 1980–1 the figure was 7.3 per cent (Piachaud, 1982).

Piachaud also demonstrates that, between 1950–1 and 1980–1, women's earnings increased more rapidly than men's. Wives contribute 21 per cent to the after-tax incomes of their families (Fry and Morris, 1984) without which the overall standard of living of their husbands and their children would be considerably lower. Access to owner occupied housing for example, often depends on a period when a couple are both earning and can afford to save for a deposit and then meet the initial high mortgage repayments. At a time of public sector housing cuts, this is of increasing importance. Thus, we have arrived at a situation where: 'If mothers stay at home to care for their children ... then families will experience lower living standards than those enjoyed by the childless.' (Piachaud, 1982, p. 19.)

The increase in women's earnings in relation to men's was largely a phenomenon of the early and mid-1970s and demonstrates the impact of the 1970 Equal Pay Act (implemented from 1975) and incomes policies favouring low paid workers. The economic penalties suffered by families with only one earner are particularly glaring in Britain, since most other European countries are more generous in their endowment of children than Britain. In addition several countries are prepared to pay for mothers to stay at home to care for young children. France has a special allowance for families with a single breadwinner, and Hungary introduced grants in 1967 for mothers who stay at home to care for children under three. In chapter 7 we shall examine debates within feminism as to whether such an approach to care is desirable. Here, we are merely concerned to note that, whilst the State argues that mothers *should* stay at home to care for children, it is not prepared to pay to make that a realistic option for most families.

As women have become a more significant part of the labour force, we have seen some trade unions as well as the EEC and women's organizations promoting women's rights at work, for example, the right to return to their job after maternity leave. Whilst there has been some attack on these rights in recent years, they nevertheless represent advances, albeit limited, for women at work, and pressure from the EEC is likely to hold the line against a wholesale dismantling of such rights. It is all the more ironic then, that the present Government, committed as it is to such a strong 'traditional family' approach, should have if anything widened the gap between those who conform to their ideology that mothers should stay at home, and those who don't – with those who conform coming off worst.

Part III:

Feminist strategies to change welfare

7

The economic position of women – alternative perspectives

The best things in life may be free, but the phrase has a hollow ring for most women who provide most free services for others, and have least leisure time for enjoying the wider pleasures of life. Whether they are unpaid housewives, or low paid wage workers most women lack money. To avoid poverty, they must link themselves to a male breadwinner, and marriage thus becomes their most promising career in terms of financial rewards. Amongst those without attachment to a male breadwinner, such as single parent families, poverty is widespread.

In this chapter, we shall examine conflicting perspectives within the women's movement on how the goal of financial independence for women can be won. We shall concentrate on the position of the majority of women – i.e. working-class women. The expansion of higher education over the past twenty years has increased the number of women entering well paid careers, particularly in the public sector. There are still areas of professional work where women are grossly underrepresented: engineering, the law, higher management, for example, and we shall see in chapter 8 how organizations such as the Equal Opportunities Commission promote projects in schools to encourage girls to take traditionally male subjects and widen their career opportunities. These are not unimportant, but however successful they are, they will have little impact on the economic position of the majority of women, who in capitalist society have little prospect of such careers. How have feminists responded to their interests?

Paid work – inside or outside the home?

Most feminists can probably agree over what is wrong with women's present economic position. Women are exploited in waged work because they are used as a cheap and flexible workforce. Women are exploited in the home because they provide free caring services for husbands, children and adult dependants. Feminists disagree, however, on how to end this double exploitation. In particular, some feminists place greater emphasis on improving women's position in the labour market, whilst others believe that the central issue is for women to have an income from the State for the work they do at home.

Strategies to improve women's position in the labour market involve a range of liberal, reformist and socialist demands for equal pay with men, ending sex discrimination in the labour market, and paying some form of minimum wage. Socialist feminists take this strategy a step further, since they argue that women's position in the home enables capitalists to use them as a reserve army of labour. We shall be looking at these demands in more detail later. Here it is necessary simply to point out that these approaches presuppose that the central issue is how women can achieve full participation in the labour market alongside men.

The Marxist tradition, to which most socialist feminists relate in some way, has always emphasized the progressive implications of women's participation in waged work. Engels, Marx's contemporary and collaborator, argued that women's liberation depended on taking all women out of the home and into public industry.

Most socialist feminists today are rather critical of Engels' naive assumption that once women were absorbed into factory work, the sexual division of labour in the home would disappear and men's patriarchal attitudes and behaviour would wither away. Many would also take issue with his rather simplistic view that large-scale factory production, because it is *social* rather than private, and because it uses 'modern' technology, is somehow 'better' than the primitive home. We are much more sensitive today to the negative aspects of technology and large-scale enterprise both in relation to human beings and the ecological balance of our world. Himmelweit points out that certain aspects of domestic work, such as the lack of a boss standing over you and controlling your work, are positive in comparison with waged work. She argues that: 'we should be attempting to create new relations for all work, in which those of domestic labour and those of wage labour which are the more humanizing are blended . . .' (Himmelweit, 1983, p. 125).

Despite these criticisms of the traditional Marxist approach to wage labour, it remains true that the main thrust of socialist feminist thinking on women's economic position tends to be around the issue of how women can improve their labour market position. It is assumed that women want to work outside the home, that this is progressive and that the key problem is how to introduce changes both in the workplace and the home which will enable women to do so. Most socialist feminists recognize the need for an autonomous women's movement, since the labour movement is male dominated. However, they recognize that the main agent for change in workplace practices is the trade union movement. They therefore encourage women to participate in the trade union movement, and attempt to change union policies from within, as well as through the autonomous campaigns of the women's movement.

A very different approach to that of both liberal and socialist feminists is offered by women such as Selma James and the Power of Women Collective who advocate 'wages for housework'. The idea of wages for housework developed out of a pamphlet first published in 1972 by the Italian feminist Mariarosa Dalla Costa and the American/British Selma James. They agree with socialist feminists that women's super-exploitation as wage workers arises from their responsibility for unpaid domestic labour. Unlike socialist feminists, however, they see women's central struggle as being at home and in the community, around domestic labour, rather than in the labour market. In the original 1972 article the authors argue that women should refuse to do housework, and should instead get involved in community struggles around issues such as housing, nursery provision and schools. This is explicitly posed as an alternative to the idea of women seeking paid work outside the home. In a section entitled 'Women and the Struggle Not to Work' this is spelt out very clearly:

Up to now, the myth of female incapacity, rooted in this isolated woman dependent on someone else's wage and therefore shaped by someone else's consciousness, has been

broken by only one action: the woman getting her own wage
... performing social labor in a socialised structure, whether
the factory or the office, and initiating there her own forms of
social rebellion along with the traditional forms of the class.
*The advent of the women's movement is a rejection of this
alternative.*   (Dalla Costa and James, 1972, p. 47)

The rejection of the work ethic and the priority given to
community struggles as opposed to the organized labour
movement mirrors the resurgence of libertarian community
activism in the late 1960s and early 1970s. The approach has been
very much influenced by feminists from Italy where this current is
particularly strong. Since then, the theory and practice have been
developed in two ways. In the first place, Selma James and those
around her have adopted the slogan of 'wages for housework' to
express the idea that housework is *work* and that women should
not have to work outside the home in order to make ends meet.
Second, James has developed an explicit analysis of trade unions,
whom she regards as totally reactionary since they are part of the
capitalist system, defending the interests of those who are already
privileged in the division of labour, white men, at the expense of
black people and women: 'The struggle of the women of the
working class against the union is so decisive because, like the
family, *it protects 'the class' at her expense* ... (James, 1976,
p. 10).

The unions are unequivocally assigned by James to the dustbin
of history. In contrast, Michele Barrett, a socialist feminist, is
almost apologetic at having to make yet another criticism of the
trade unions:

Many socialist feminists feel that the weight of feminist
arguments has been mainly criticial. ... After a while, these
criticisms, however justified they may be, can often be seen as
undermining ones.

We are educating a generation of young feminists into the
belief that the organisations of the left are irretrievably locked
into a sexism as bad as that of any other men, and alienating
the mass of ordinary working people who might otherwise be
brought to support an egalitarian approach to women.
                                        (Barrett, 1981b, p. 36)

While Barrett sees the charge that feminists are 'undermining'
as misplaced, the tone of her article nevertheless shows the

importance she attaches to attempting to influence male trade unionists in a progressive direction, rather than seeing the struggle as *against* them.

At a theoretical level, Selma James' ideas are close to those of many Marxist feminists. In particular, she emphasizes that women's domestic labour benefits capitalism. Thus, the demand for wages for housework is related to the question of *strategy*. In this respect the Power of Women Collective are closer to radical feminists in their stress on the need for women to develop their own power and autonomy from men and male dominated institutions.

Having looked at the central, strategic division within feminism, we shall now look in more detail at the range of proposals put forward by feminists to give women economic independence, and the problems and contradictions thrown up by the campaigns of the women's movement. We shall first look at the position of women in the home, and then at labour market policies.

An income for women at home

In chapter 6 we saw how state income maintenance policies treat the household as the unit of assessment, in which women are assumed to be dependent on men. Almost all feminists argue that social security benefits should be unpicked – 'disaggregated' – so that women and men can each claim benefit in their own right. Aspects of this approach command wide support both in the WLM and outside. Thus the 'poverty lobby' and the Claimants Union have campaigned against the cohabitation rule and the WLM launched two campaigns for disaggregation in the mid-1970s: in 1975 the London Women's Liberation Campaign for Legal and Financial Independence (LWLCLFI) was set up and in 1977 the 'YBA Wife' Campaign was launched. Such organizations have been involved in traditional pressure group activity, submitting evidence to official enquiries, for example, as well as campaigning as part of the WLM. They have argued, principally, that tax allowances and social security benefits should be allocated to people as *individuals*. This means that regardless of the type of household in which people live, individuals should receive the same allowances and benefits – there should be no 'single person's allowance' or 'married man's allowance', simply a single adult person's allowance. Similarly, the scale rate for a married couple on Supplementary Benefit should simply be the aggregate of the claims made by two individuals, no different from the claims made by two single people. This would enable the wives of working husbands to claim in their own right.

The demand for disaggregation is essentially an equal rights demand concerned with the form of social security benefits. It is radical because it challenges the idea of women's dependence on men and of the nuclear family. In practice, disaggregation involves a lot more than simply treating married/cohabiting women with children as financially independent from their partners. At present, men and single women without children have to 'sign on' as available for work in order to claim benefit. Feminists' intention is not to force women with children to look for work, but to give them the choice of staying at home to look after children without thereby becoming dependent on a male breadwinner. Disaggregation is not, therefore, a change that can be implemented without a fundamental review of the way the social security system treats parents, and how it relates to the labour market – a non-sexist scheme would give men the option of staying at home to care for children, whilst many married women undertaking low-paid, part-time work might prefer not to do so if they had an income in their own right from the State.

This last argument is central to the Power of Women Collective's demand for wages for housework. They argue that, if women at home received a wage, they would no longer be forced to take on menial, low paid work. The reduction in the number of women seeking work would then force employers to provide better pay and conditions for those who remained in the labour market. The group's focus on *housework* is, however, unacceptable to most feminists. The issue is not housework *per se*, but the socially necessary work of caring for dependants.

Today, the demand for wages for housework is rarely heard in the women's movement, but the wider issue of whether women should campaign for payment for undertaking work in the home is still a live issue. In chapter 6 we outlined the feminist critique of community care, and the arguments in favour of some form of care *in* the community rather than care *by* the community. This might be construed as involving making all caring, at least of adult dependants, paid work outside the family – in residential homes and day centres, or through the paid work of home helps, district nurses and other workers. On the other hand, millions of women are caring, without pay, for dependants at home, and their lives would be significantly improved if they received an independent income. Fairbairns argues that looking after dependants is socially necessary work, which should be paid for by society through wages – whether to women (or men) in the home, or to the employees of local authorities, voluntary organizations or indeed, commercial caring agencies (Fairbairns, 1981). Rights of Women (ROW) proposes a system of Home Responsibility Payments payable to those who care for adult dependants regardless of whether or not they are in paid work (ROW 1979). This would improve the economic position of carers. At present married women are excluded from receiving Invalid Care Allowance altogether, and single women have to have given up paid work. On the other hand, it would not necessarily alter the situation whereby many women feel pressured into taking responsibility for elderly dependants who need full-time care, unless of course the payment was sufficiently high to tempt men to compete with women to take on this role, hardly a likely scenario.

An alternative approach is to make payments directly available to those who *need* care, rather than to those who provide it. Elderly or disabled people, for example, could thereby purchase the services of carers rather than relying on a single carer in their family. In practice this would mean massively extending the coverage and value of the present Attendance Allowance. In theory, this should end the pressure on individual female relatives to take on physical caring, since those in need could purchase services provided by the market, the State, or voluntary organizations. However, it seems unlikely that the level of any proposed benefit would be high enough to enable the majority of elderly and disabled people to purchase sufficient of the range of services they would need if they were to avoid relying on their relatives. Furthermore, a system which relied primarily on providing those in need with *incomes* would only help women if institutions such as local authorities or commercial organizations actually provided the range of services which the elderly needed to purchase. In practice we might doubt whether the size of any proposed benefit would be sufficient to make the venture profitable, or whether local authorities would make sufficient investment in such services, knowing that those in need could simply pay relatives to care for them. For these reasons, some feminists may argue that, whatever the merits of these proposals, at the end of the day they undermine attempts to press the State for more collective provisions rather than relying on individual carers.

In practice feminists are often less than consistent in their attitudes to this issue. Bennett argues that:

Feminists have not argued against the extension of invalid care
allowance on the grounds that this would be paying women to
stay at home. Yet we would expect these arguments to be
advanced automatically if the government suggested wages for
full-time child-care by mothers.

(Bennet, 1983, p. 206)

This inconsistency should not necessarily be seen as a weakness in
feminism. The search for a single, logically consistent approach
may be illusory for two reasons. First, feminist campaigns need to
have a long term goal of transforming all gendered relationships
of domination and subordination in society. This may well entail
abolishing the role of full-time, individual carer, in favour of a
variety of forms of collective care in which both sexes play a role.
In the meantime, feminism needs to have something to offer to
women today. In a situation where millions of women are caring
for dependants with little or no money of their own, we ignore at
our peril their grievances when denied Invalid Care Allowance or
their anger at the low level of Child Benefit. One of the most
successful campaigns of the women's movement was in defence of
Family Allowances. In 1972, the Conservative Government
published a green paper advocating a system of tax credits which
would replace Family Allowances with credits paid into men's
pay packets. A campaign against these proposals received massive
support from women who signed petitions, and in some cases
joined sit-ins in post offices. To many women in the wages for
housework campaign, this confirmed their perspective. Suzie
Fleming argued that 'The Family Allowance Campaign has given
political expression to the idea of extending payment from the
state for work women already do, work in the home.' (Fleming
1975, p. 12.) We do not, however, have to agree with wages for
housework to appreciate that defending women's income from the
State is a necessary part of defending women's immediate,
material interests.

A second reason why the search for complete consistency in
our demands may be illusory is that the significance of any piece
of social policy depends not just on its formal provisions but on
whether the change was won as a result of struggle or was
imposed from above. An income for non-working mothers over
and above the present meagre Child Benefit which was won as a
result of struggles by the women's movement to improve women's
lives would be very different from a benefit introduced by a pro-
natalist Government, which intended to remove women from the
labour market and confine them to the home.

Women and the labour market

Social policies which provided women with an income for work in the home would, as we have already argued, influence women's position in the labour market. Nevertheless, state income maintenance policies cannot in themselves be the route to changing the low paid position of women in the labour market. Direct action is needed, either through equal pay legislation, policies to help low paid workers, or attempts to provide women with greater opportunities in the labour market.

In 1970, Britain's Equal Pay Act was passed, making it illegal for employers to pay women less than men doing the same or broadly similar job, or assessed as being of equal value under a job evaluation scheme. Since only a very small number of workers were affected by job evaluation schemes, employers had plenty of leeway to avoid equal pay on the grounds that men and women were doing different jobs. The problem was exacerbated by the provision of a delay of five years between the passing of the legislation and its coming into force. Many employers took advantage of this delay to introduce re-grading or changes in job content which would enable them to argue that men and women were doing different work. (See for example, Glucklich and Snell, undated.)

Where a woman believes she is entitled to equal pay under the Act, she can take her case to an Industrial Tribunal. Under the original provisions of the Act, she had to prove that she was doing 'like work' to a man, and that there was no 'material difference' other than difference in sex, between her case and his. Such a procedure was inevitably daunting to many women, and the number of successful cases has been small. The majority were either withdrawn or dismissed by the tribunals, who often took an extremely narrow interpretation of 'like work'. The EOC cites the case, for example, of women who assembled spouts for car radiators who were refused equal pay with men who, as spout repairers, did virtually the same job only in reverse order. Not surprisingly, the number of claims has dropped from 1,742 in 1976 to only 39 in 1982.

These criticisms of legislation have made many feminists sceptical of the value of legislation – it may even undermine women's fight for equality if they are told 'You have the Equal Pay Act – what are you complaining about?' Nevertheless, many argue that legislation *is* valuable, although it is not sufficient to achieve equal pay. In particular, the existence of legislation may strengthen the bargaining position of trade union negotiators

representing women workers, and form a base from which to
press for more effective legislation. Thus the EOC and the NCCL
have been in the forefront of attempts to improve the legislation,
in particular by the substitution of 'work of equal value' for 'like
work'. In this, they have been greatly helped by the EEC Court
of Justice Ruling of July 1982, which required the British
government to amend the 1970 Act to provide for equal pay for
work of equal value. The new regulations were introduced in
January 1984 and have led to an upsurge in the number of equal
pay claims. Nevertheless, the procedures are still far from
satisfactory and the EOC is continuing to press for legal
regulations less obviously stacked against women.

During the early and mid-1970s the gap between men and
women's earnings narrowed from 63 per cent in 1970 to 75.5 per
cent in 1977. Some women have argued that this was not
primarily due to the Equal Pay Act, but to the impact of incomes
policies which were biased in favour of low paid workers. Since
the majority of women workers are low paid, and women form
the majority of low paid workers, it makes sense to improve
women's position through a strategy towards low pay rather than
sex equality as such. Such a strategy could revolve around
legislation for a minimum wage, or some form of incomes policy.

Neither minimum wage legislation nor incomes policy have
found much favour in the trade union movement generally, or
with the political left. Many trade unionists argue that a statutory
minimum wage undermines trade union organization since
workers have less reason to join unions if their wages are
externally regulated, and that the minimum wage tends to become
a maximum – the low rates of pay in industries covered by Wages
Councils which fix minimum rates of pay in certain industries are
often cited as proof of this maxim. Similarly, both Marxists and
trade unionists have argued that incomes policy benefits capital
not the low paid, since workers in profitable industries tend to
forego wage increases, but wages for the low paid, or social
benefits for the working class generally receive no compensating
boost.

These arguments appear neutral as regards gender – they refer
only to the interests of the working class. Some socialist feminists,
however, argue that to refer to 'class interests' in this way masks
the real differences of interest that exist between men and women
workers. In particular, Beatrix Campbell argued in two articles in
1978 and 1980 that women had benefited from the incomes
policies of the early 1970s which were biased in favour of low
paid workers, and that the return to free collective bargaining in

1978 was associated with a widening of the gap between men's and women's wages. Free collective bargaining is the means whereby privileged workers, especially white male skilled workers, maintain their position in the wages' pecking order: 'it is not an effective socialist economic strategy against capitalism nor is it in any way a strategy for women's equality.' (Campbell and Charlton, 1981, p. 34.)

In the place of free collective bargaining, Campbell initially proposed some notion of feminist incomes policy, involving some form of national determination of wage increases, biased towards the low paid.

This analysis was extremely controversial amongst socialist feminists, and more recently, Beatrix Campbell has made her criticism of free collective bargaining somewhat more muted. The substance of her argument – against differentials and in favour of flat rate pay increases – remains unchanged, but she no longer argues that collective bargaining *per se* is the problem and stresses that she is not arguing against the *form* of collective bargaining, merely its *content* (Campbell, 1984).

Today, there is a fairly broad consensus amongst socialist feminists that what is needed is a new Alternative Economic Strategy (AES) which combines economic policies designed to improve women's position in the labour market with social policies to ensure that society rather than individual women take on responsibility for caring for dependants. Thus Angela Weir and Mary McIntosh argue for a combined strategy to end job segregation and low pay, give part-time workers the same rights as full-timers, reduce the working week and reform social services so as to give everyone individual rights to benefits in cash and kind (Weir and McIntosh, 1982).

More radically, Anna Coote argues that we should not start from questions about wages and jobs, but should ask 'how shall we care for and support our children?' In her view, the starting point for an AES is generous child care facilities, and a shorter working week to enable both parents to be involved in work outside the home and child care. Policies on pay would include a statutory minimum wage and increased child benefit (Coote, 1981).

Whatever the differences in their specific demands, socialist feminists share two points in common. They believe that we must break down the distinction between 'pay policy' and 'social policy', in favour of looking more broadly at the allocation of society's resources between classes and between men and women. Such resources include both money in the form of wages and social security benefits, and time – women will not be equal if they receive the same income as men but still perform the double shift of work inside and outside the home.

In the second place, socialist feminists are critical of the trade union movement for defending men's interests, but they nevertheless believe that women have to fight for change *within* trade unions and the left, rather than ignoring them as irretrievably male dominated. This reflects their theory that both gender *and* capitalism are the cause of women's oppression, and that the trade unions, as the defensive organizations of the working class, have a progressive role despite male dominance. Weir and McIntosh, for example, argue:

> Women could never force the trade union movement to take up our fight if there were no strong women's movement outside mobilizing women. . . . But it is important that the women's movement and the labour movement are not seen as alternatives or antagonistic . . . we must fight our battles *within* the unions themselves, not construct the whole trade union movement as irredeemable and forever our enemy.
>
> (Weir and McIntosh, 1982, p. 18)

It is probably a misnomer to speak of *the* trade union movement in Britain. Unions fall into three broad categories: the craft manual unions, the white collar unions, and the generalist manual unions. Many unions in the first group probably can be characterized as 'irredeemable' in terms of feminist politics. But many unions in the second group have predominantly female memberships, whilst the latter represent low paid men and women and share women's interest in seeing minimum wage legislation and flat rate wage increases. At the grass roots level, women *have* been struggling in their unions and we have seen both successes and setbacks. The great problem ahead is whether women can make any impact at *national* level in transforming the AES from a programme for men to one for *all*. As Anna Coote points out, '(feminist) proposals cannot simply be added on to the existing strategy, because they will not work unless they are given political priority'. (Coote, 1981, p. 7.)

At the present time women have a long way to go before *their* priorities will become labour movement priorities.

Conclusion

If women are to get their fair share of society's resources – both financial resources and leisure time – a totally new approach has to be adopted to the relationship between economic and social policy. It is no use talking about full employment if women cannot take on paid work because of their responsibilities for the care of dependants. Equally, it is necessary for society to recognize that caring carried out in the home is work which is just as important to society as the manufacture of motor cars or the generation of electricity. At the end of the day, feminist demands mean that the division between economic and social policies must be ended in favour of a broad perspective on social priorities in the sphere of both production and reproduction. Whichever specific strategy is adopted, it must involve a massive increase in the share of society's resources devoted to those who care for our dependants.

The problem feminists face in achieving this goal is that our demands are bound to meet with opposition from all sides. The State and capital will not support giving more resources to carers: the State would face an enormous budget deficit if it could no longer rely on women's unpaid labour of love, whilst the capitalist economy would be adversely affected by the measures which the State would need to take in order to raise the revenues needed to meet this deficit. Whilst most men may support women in seeking payments for carers since this would increase family incomes, they are unlikely to favour any measures which involve a redistribution of income from men to women. At a time of high unemployment, men may damage their own interests if they support women in their attempts to achieve full equality in the labour market. Although we believe that we must find spaces to work with men in anti-capitalist struggles in the labour market, and around issues such as social spending, we nevertheless believe that women's demands for choice in how they live their lives, and the work they undertake, brings them into conflict with men, the State, and capital.

8

Changing the welfare system from within

All feminists unite in regarding existing welfare institutions as unsatisfactory for women. They have also united to fight practical campaigns to reform certain aspects of these institutions. Beneath this practical unity, however, significant disagreements have emerged over how to explain women's negative experiences of welfare and what strategies to adopt in order to eliminate them. Liberal reformist feminists remain relatively optimistic that welfare institutions can be improved significantly even within existing society. On the other hand both radical and socialist feminists, albeit for rather different reasons, are sceptical of the potential for fundamental welfare improvements for all women within a patriarchal/capitalist society. Nevertheless, a significant number of women welfare workers who regard themselves as socialist or radical feminists are working and struggling within mainstream welfare institutions to develop a feminist practice. They do not believe that their activities will of themselves transform welfare services – to achieve this requires structural changes to society. But they do believe that struggling 'in and against the state' is necessary if feminists are to achieve anything in the here and now.

In this chapter we will examine two liberal/reformist strategies for change: enlightening welfare providers as to how their existing behaviour is sexist, how it affects women and how they can improve it, and campaigning for equal employment opportunities for women in the welfare professions. We will also look at

136

attempts by feminist welfare workers to create an explicitly feminist form of welfare practice.

Educating welfare providers

In Britain the strategy of educating welfare providers has been most vigorously pursued in the field of education, particularly by the EOC. Members of the EOC have consistently claimed that most sex discrimination which has occurred within educational institutions has been inadvertent rather than deliberate or structural. In its 1977 Annual Report, for example, the EOC defended its emphasis on informal persuasion as the best means of implementing the education sections of the Sex Discrimination Act on the grounds that 'Authorities and Head Teachers *may not have realised* (our emphasis) the implications of continuing the traditional practice of segregating the sexes for (certain) subjects.' (EOC, 1977, p. 25.) As well as holding talks with key policy makers in the educational field the EOC has therefore concentrated on influencing the attitudes and practices of classroom teachers by holding special conferences and courses for teachers to promote key issues relating to women and education, and by producing a wide range of promotional and teaching material for teachers, schools, parents and pupils. In 1979, for example, the EOC published a booklet aimed at schools entitled 'Do You Provide Equal Educational Opportunities?' in which suggestions were given 'for the elimination of sex discrimination in education and training and the positive promotion of equality of opportunity'. In this booklet the EOC stressed that 'the vast majority of cases of sex discrimination in education and training occur by default' and gave the object of the booklet as 'to make everyone concerned with education and training aware of the legislation so that "discrimination by default" can be eradicated'. The booklet sets out detailed guidelines giving 'practical suggestions for the development of educational initiatives which will provide a sound basis for real equality of opportunity'. (EOC, 1979, p. 4.)

In recent years the EOC has expressed particular interest in the problem of female pupils failing to break through in significant numbers in 'male' careers such as computer science, engineering and technology. In 1984 the EOC co-operated with the Engineering Council to launch WISE 84 (Women Into Science and Engineering) which was intended to 'stimulate the development of projects in all sectors of education and industry to encourage girls and women to pursue careers in engineering, science and technology.' (EOC, 1984.) The EOC's main role in relation to WISE was to disseminate guidelines and special information packs to primary and secondary schools and to encourage schools to set up special projects. The EOC has now supported an impressive array of initiatives and projects to combat sex discrimination in schools. It would be impossible to find the space here even to list these activities, but in 1981 the EOC itself summarized just some of the larger initiatives which it was supporting:

> Some progress is being made in a number of areas, among them Tameside, where girls are grouped together specifically for mathematics; Manchester, where a four year intervention project of 'Girls into Science and Technology' aims to ensure the active participation of girls in these subjects: Clwyd, where the local authority has established with the EOC a two year research project into sex discrimination in secondary schools within the area. (Carr, 1981, p. 10)

Whilst the EOC has produced a great deal of documentary evidence of its attempts gently to persuade educators to abandon all sexist thoughts and habits there is very little documentary evidence on similar close and co-operative links between feminists and other welfare professionals. Ruzek's remarkably comprehensive account of the American Women's Health Movement only mentions, briefly, that in the mid-1970s some American women's health groups did attempt to influence male doctors directly by going into medical schools to teach medical students about women's health care needs. But the only specific example Ruzek gives of this co-operative educational approach is that of the women's Community Health Centre based in Cambridge, Massachusetts, which set up a programme to teach male medical students how to perform pelvic examinations in a way which would not hurt or degrade or patronize their patients. However, the women ceased working with male medical students in 1976 on the grounds, according to Ruzek, that feminists should insist on self help and reciprocal sharing in medical care and that 'men cannot share in a pelvic examination.' (Ruzek, 1978, p. 152.)

In Britain the EOC has paid very little attention to women's health care – presumably because it has no statutory role in relation to the NHS, but some feminist doctors have played a very active role in the campaign for Well Women Clinics (see chapter 9) and have no doubt spent much time personally trying to persuade some of their less than enthusiastic colleagues of the validity of the feminist critique of conventional medical services for women. Similarly, individual feminist academics have given occasional lectures to medical students on women's health care issues and feminist social work lecturers may now devote even more time to giving social work students a feminist perspective on their future profession.

A sex change for welfare providers

A key liberal feminist strategy in relation to welfare services has been to campaign vigorously for equal career opportunities for women within the welfare professions. This strategy has had a dual objective. To increase career opportunities for women (mainly white middle-class women) and to reduce the sexist nature of welfare institutions.

In the fields of education and social work liberal/reformist feminists have placed considerable emphasis on campaigns designed to encourage female teachers and social workers to apply for positions of authority and power. The EOC has also fought against men's continuing attempts to discriminate against those women who do apply for such positions. The EOC clearly regards its emphasis on career opportunities for female welfare professionals as benefiting women both as workers and as welfare clients. According to Eileen Byrne, one-time Education Officer to the EOC, for example,

> It is crucial that both girls and boys actually *see* women in leadership, management, government, making decisions in their daily lives, if we are to break the cycle of under-achievement. As long as children see men taking the top posts, decisions and higher pay and women tacitly accepting this ... children will believe what they see and not what we say.
>
> (Byrne, 1978, p. 212)

Feminists have used similar arguments in relation to social work. In 1980 Ruth Popplestone pointed out, with the aid of statistical evidence, that there were negligible numbers of women at the top of the social work hierarchy and suggested that the lack of women at senior management level in Social Services Departments might be partly responsible for those features of social work management such as 'lack of humanity, putting administrative concerns before client welfare and bureaucracy' which attract so much complaint. She concluded 'There is no intrinsic reason why the more human qualities cannot be developed by men, but they are more likely under present conditions to be found in women' (Popplestone, 1980, p. 15). Whereas in education and social work contemporary feminists have campaigned primarily to get women into top positions, in medicine they have had to fight first of all to get a significant number of women into medical schools and the basic career grades.

Even reformist feminists usually accept that where women are allowed to participate in a male world in only token numbers, they are likely to deal with the severe 'cognitive and emotional dissonance' by thinking and acting as much like their male colleagues as possible. This, they argue, explains why some women doctors have related to their female patients in overtly patronizing and even sexist ways. Many feminists are optimistic, however, that the increasing numbers of women doctors in most areas of medicine will enable women to support each other, stand up against institutionalized sexism and fight for more radical change. Seaman reports that it is now well established that:

> When women enter (male preserves) in sufficient numbers to provide each other with a significant female peer group (15 per cent to one third appears adequate) most are able to rest comfortably with their female identity and to question generalisations and clichés about women as a class instead of deeming themselves exceptional.   (Seaman, 1975a, p. 44)

Some feminists have claimed that a large increase in the number of female doctors will in itself significantly improve the health care given to female patients. A few radical feminists have taken the demand for more women physicians as a means of improving women's health care to its logical limits. In 1975 Barbara Seaman told a conference on women and health that in future male medical students should be barred from obstetrics and gynaecology. 'It sounds a bit radical at first', she said, smiling, 'but you get used to it.' (Seaman, 1975b, p. 14.)

Creating feminist welfare practice within mainstream services

A growing number of women welfare professionals are struggling to work within mainstream social services either on their own or with the support of feminist colleagues, in ways intended to create new forms of welfare practice based on feminist principles. In 1981, for example, Gail Young, a feminist doctor, claimed that an increasing number of women doctors were beginning to criticize conventional medicine from within and concluded that women health workers as well as consumers had a responsibility to fight for 'a health service which is caring and egalitarian, reflects our needs and aspirations as women and the new values which women and feminism can provide'. (Young, 1981, p. 162.)

Within social work, feminists such as Judy Hale and Annie Hudson are now exploring what a feminist social work practice might actually be like. They both suggest that in dealing with female clients feminist social workers can work in ways which assist women to recognize their own strengths and to then reinforce those strengths. They give practical examples of these ways of working with clients and suggest that rather than blaming individual women for their 'failure' as wives or mothers feminist social workers should suggest to these women that many of their problems result from structural constraints on their lives, particularly in relation to the family. They warn feminist social workers, however, to avoid giving clients the impression that they are so oppressed that nothing can be changed and emphasize that even within existing society individual women in need can be helped by feminist social work practice. According to Annie Hudson:

> All women are conscious ... of some of the inequities of women's position in our society; they do not need social workers to tell them that. But what social workers can do is offer support to women in enhancing their confidence and capacity to be assertive in handling the world, whether this is at home, at the local DHSS office or elsewhere. (Hudson, 1984.)

Radical feminists such as Dale Spender, whilst still struggling to put their feminist principles into practice in their own classrooms, seminar groups and lectures, are now so sceptical of the potential for major changes within male dominated education institutions that they have proposed the setting up of separatist explicitly feminist girls' schools, women's colleges and even universities. Whilst recognizing the value of the insights which have led radical feminists to such drastic conclusions we see little evidence to suggest that separatist feminist schools or colleges funded by the State could be a viable proposition in the foreseeable future. A more reformist approach to this separatist issue which has now been adopted by a number of British feminists working within the mainstream education system is the defence of existing single-sex secondary schools and the setting up within mixed schools of separate classes for girls for certain traditionally male subjects. This strategy has the advantage of enabling feminist teachers to put their principles into practice within existing schools without having to fight off the constant attempts by boys in mixed classes to hog their attention. It might also enable girls to study those subjects at which they have traditionally achieved less than boys without being distracted by the presence of their sometimes less than gentlemanly rivals.

Ironically, while some practising feminist teachers are exploring the possibility of dividing boys and girls for certain subjects, others are attempting to put their principles into practice by discouraging any divisions between the sexes. Delamont reports the practice of a deputy head of a primary school whose 'Ten Ways to Counter Sexism' include:

> I never even for the slightest convenience divide the children into boys and girls for any activity

as well as:

> I never co-operate with teachers' requests for 'four strong boys to move these boxes please'. I train the girls to lift and carry – very difficult at first

and

> In sewing and cookery which the boys do I always opposed suggestions that the boys will grow up homosexual by asking why this would be such a bad thing anyway (Delamont, 1980, pp. 11–12).

What have feminists achieved?

The empirical evidence

The EOC has now spent eight years working co-operatively with educational policy makers and teachers to reduce sex discrimination in the education system. According to its own staff much progress has been made in a 'short time'. In 1983 its Principal Education Officer claimed that:

In 7 years a great deal has been achieved. Seven years is not even one generation of school children and in that time equal opportunities have moved from the margins to the mainstream of education debate. . . . Where once the E.O.C. was regarded by some as extreme, its concerns as marginal, now we are unable to meet all the demands made upon us for funding and we are having to work hard to keep ourselves informed of all the initiatives which are taking place.   (EOC, 1983a, p. 6)

The EOC has collected a significant amount of empirical evidence to back up their claim that the position of women in education is changing, slowly perhaps, but steadily and in the right direction. As far as women teachers are concerned the EOC claims that overt or direct discrimination against women applying for headships may no longer be the key factor behind women's continuing under-representation at the top. Liberal feminists now argue that more complex factors such as the conflicts for women between work and family life and women's reluctance to move from caring jobs into management now play an important role in perpetuating men's dominance at the top of all welfare professions (see for example Popplestone, 1980). Nevertheless liberal/reformist feminists remain optimistic that affirmative action programmes such as those already implemented in the USA could have a significant effect on female welfare professionals' career opportunities.

Recent action by ILEA has certainly demonstrated that a practical commitment to being an 'equal opportunities' employer – as opposed to simply paying lip-service to the principle – can have a positive effect on women teachers' careers.

As far as women as consumers of education are concerned liberal feminists emphasize that examination statistics now show significant improvements in girls' scientific achievements. In 1974 girls gained only 21.9 per cent of 'A' level passes in Pure and Applied Maths and only 18.4 per cent of 'A' level passes in Physics (EOC, 1981a). By 1982 girls were gaining 29.3 per cent of passes in 'A' level maths and 20.5 per cent of 'A' level passes in physics. Statistics, however, do not all support an optimistic view of girls' recent educational gains. Some subjects remain rigidly 'male' or 'female'. In 1982 99 per cent of 'A' level candidates in domestic science subjects were girls, while only 3 per cent of entrants for 'O' level design and technology were girls. This final figure is particularly disturbing since, as Martin Grant has pointed out, individuals with no understanding of technology will increasingly have to rely on technical experts not only for simple repairs but also for taking decisions which will affect the very nature of our future society. According to Grant, women who are denied an adequate technological education are effectively disenfranchised from the increasingly important politics of technology, as well as losing out on a growing range of career opportunities (Grant, 1983).

Liberal/reformist feminists claim that although women are still not completely equal with men in the education field this can be primarily explained by the complexity of the problem and by the time it takes to implement effective reforms. Many local education authorities and individual schools, the EOC insists, are now firmly committed to encouraging girls to take more interest in science and technology but it will take several years for this new positive approach to be reflected in 'A' level statistics and the proportion of women taking scientific and technological degrees. Liberal feminists also emphasize that whilst overt discrimination against women in education is in decline, women themselves still frequently display negative attitudes towards traditionally male subjects and these attitudes are particularly resistant to attempts to modify them. For example, in 1982 the EOC's annual report stated that:

> It is becoming increasingly clear that a number of factors which are outside the control of the school system play a very influential part in pupils' choice of examination subject options and subsequent careers. Among these factors are the influence of parents and peer groups. (EOC, 1982, p. 16)

We do not wish to undervalue the important work being done by the EOC in encouraging educators to take the issue of sex discrimination in schools seriously but we must warn readers to interpret 'optimistic' evidence with some caution. For example a postal survey, carried out by ILEA in 1982, of all its 1,115 schools found that 72 per cent of secondary schools, 53 per cent of primary schools and 79 per cent of nursery schools were taking measures to promote equal opportunities between the sexes (EOC, 1983b). However, there are at least three main grounds for treating such positive news with caution. First, ILEA has been one of the most active local education authorities in promoting equal opportunities programmes in its schools, and knowledge of this commitment to sexual equality may well have influenced the replies sent in by school heads. Second, the 10 per cent of schools which did not respond to the survey may well have been much less interested in sex discrimination in education. Third, what teachers say they are doing and what actually occurs may vary significantly. For example, researchers in Clwyd discussing sex discrimination with teachers met one headteacher who claimed 'There is no sexism in my school' but who later revealed that the head of physics objected to girls in his 'O' level class, his home economics department would not teach boys after the second year and his female deputy 'looks after visitors and refreshments because that's a woman's job.' (EOC, 1983b, p. 26.)

Similarly, whilst we fully support those feminist teachers who are struggling to create explicitly feminist teaching materials and classroom practices we should note that socialist and radical feminist teachers have themselves pointed out the very strong opposition they have encountered from male colleagues and male pupils and the press. When *Spare Rib* published an article in which the deputy head quoted earlier outlined her ten point plan to counter sexism in a junior school it provoked a backlash in the popular press and a row in the village in which she worked. (See Delamont, 1980.)

According to Delamont 'the teacher who wanted to change the ways in which schools structure sex roles for staff and pupils is liable to suffer the same reality shock as teachers with any other non-traditional ideas.' (Delamont, 1980, p. 82.)

We should not be totally negative, however, about the effects of feminist teachers' struggles within mainstream education. Recent feminist research into interactions between teachers and pupils has demonstrated that both groups are free to exercise considerable autonomy over at least certain aspects of their day-to-day school experiences. Neither feminist teachers nor female pupils can be simplistically categorized as passive victims of a totally patriarchal and oppressive system. Individual women and girls can and do work out their own strategies for coping with, resisting and ultimately perhaps fighting against sexist, oppressive policies and practices. (See Davies, 1983.)

We should emphasize that the education system does contain contradictions and that there is therefore scope for a range of responses to the dominant educational ideology.

According to Walker and Barton:

Descriptions of gender relations in education which fail to recognise that patriarchal ideologies may be contested by teachers, that curricular definitions and pedagogical practices may be challenged by pupils, that educational work roles may be redefined by academics, can only provide partial understanding.   (Walker and Barton, 1983, p. 16)

There are a number of reasons why it is more difficult to assess the degree of change within the fields of medicine and social work compared with education. First, the relationship between doctors and their patients and social workers and their clients is a much more private affair than the relationship between teachers and their pupils. Second, the outcome of 'sexist' health care or social work is particularly difficult to measure or evaluate. For example, the humiliation and frustration so vividly described by individual women who have encountered particularly sexist members of the medical profession can no more easily be measured than the pain felt by a woman undergoing a clumsy or aggressive pelvic examination. Third, the individual efforts of feminist doctors and social workers to educate their colleagues and students have yet to be quantified or systematically recorded. Finally, partly perhaps because of the difficulties outlined above, we simply do not have any quantifiable data on the extent to which medical care and social work practice have or have not become less sexist over the last few years.

The liberal campaign to get a fair proportion of women into medical schools has now achieved considerable success but the radical feminist goal of creating an all female profession of gynaecology and obstetrics is still a pipedream. In 1981 only 6 per cent of consultant obstetricians and gynaecologists working for the NHS were female (2 per cent *less* than in 1976), and only 2 per cent of senior registrars in these specialities were female (Harrison and Gretton 1984). There is some evidence that since a larger proportion of women have entered medical schools female medical students have successfully complained about overt displays of sexism by their – predominantly male – lecturers. According to Mary Ann Elston, a protest from women students at one medical school led to the complete removal of a lecturer from a particular course. Elston also reports that a number of medical textbooks have become less sexist in the last fifteen years. On the other hand there is evidence that in certain medical schools feminist criticism of medicine is still dismissed as extremist nonsense. A leading feminist expert on health care recently suggested to one group of young medical students that women giving birth might prefer to be addressed by their names rather than being called 'mum'. This suggestion was totally rejected as being inspired by an unnatural antipathy towards motherhood and the lecturer was told by one of her audience that she was 'a pervert'.

As far as medical practice is concerned a very few eminent consultants, most notably the British obstetrician Peter

146

Huntingford, have listened carefully and sympathetically to women's complaints about the nature of their services and have actively supported campaigns to give female patients the right to more choice and control over their medical treatment. However, as Peter Huntingford has pointed out most of his colleagues are still vehemently opposed to the concept of 'a woman's right to choose' on issues such as abortion and obstetric care. In 1984 a survey of GPs found that only a third agreed that abortion should be given 'on demand'. As well as statistical evidence such as this, feminists working in the field of health care continue to hear too many 'horror stories' from women who have received sexist treatment or advice from GPs and consultants – of both sexes – to be able to be optimistic about the extent to which the medical profession as a whole has responded positively to feminist pressure for change.

Those feminist social workers who are just beginning to develop new ways of working with female clients emphasize that feminist social work practice is still in its infancy and that most of their colleagues continue to treat women clients in traditional, implicitly or even overtly sexist ways. They also point out that whilst Social Service Departments continue to be controlled by men, feminist social workers will continue to face considerable opposition to the spread of new ways of working based on explicitly feminist principles and theories about the causes of women clients' problems. Nevertheless, we would suggest that because the social work profession is predominantly female and because many of those who train social workers are women, feminists may well have more scope for developing feminist welfare practice in social work institutions than in medical ones.

Radical feminists' critique of reformism

Radical feminists reject any optimistic interpretation of the effects of reformist strategies in the welfare field. There are a number of reasons for their extreme scepticism of liberal reformism. First, whereas liberal reformist feminists usually proclaim that they are not 'anti-men' and tend to explain women's negative experiences of welfare in ways which do not place all the blame on male welfare providers, radical feminists claim that sex discrimination within welfare services is not and never has been inadvertent. Rather, they accuse men of deliberately denying women an equal role, either as providers or consumers, in welfare institutions over which they have exercised total control for hundreds of years.

147

Mary Daly, for example, claims that male doctors are not simply instinctively patriarchal and patronizing towards women but that they are deeply hostile towards women in general and feminists in particular:

> the current escalation of murderous gynecological surgery (and of chemotherapy and psychotherapy) is no chronological coincidence. There is every reason to see the mutilation and destruction of women by doctors specialising in unnecessary radical masectomies and hysterectomies, carcinogenic hormone therapy, psychosurgery, spirit-killing psychiatry and other forms of psychotherapy as directly related to the rise of radical feminism in the twentieth century ... (Daly, 1979, p. 228)

Note the contrast between this and the gentle tones used by the more reformist British feminists Leeson and Gray:

> We should say straightaway that we personally have mostly experienced high standards of care and consideration from gynaecologists. So we are not opening a complaints' file, we are just noting the rather strange circumstances of doctors (mostly men) who deal exclusively with women. . . . It might seem bizarre if a woman doctor specialised in men's diseases, for example, prostatic surgery, but our society seems to accept the parallel phenomena of male gynaecologists as natural. With the best will in the world they must labour under severe disadvantages. (Leeson and Gray, 1978, p. 135.)

Second, because radical feminists are so pessimistic about men's motives towards women they insist that male welfare providers will not voluntarily give up any of their power either to female colleagues or to female clients. They may concede token gains to token women but these women will not be allowed to make any significant reforms to patriarchal medicine. Thus, according to Gena Corea most female doctors are still forced to become 'honorary white males' and fail to defend women patients against 'harmful obstetrical practices, unnecessary surgery, unsafe contraceptives and forced sterilizations.' (Corea, 1977, p. 62.) For Mary Daly even forms of psychotherapy which are overtly feminist are to be distrusted on the grounds that 'feminist' psychotherapists have been co-opted by an all pervasive patriarchy which is fundamentally oppressive to all truly radical feminists. (Daly, 1979, p. 280.) Radical feminists argue that however many women are allowed to pursue careers within male dominated welfare institutions they will never be allowed to alter the real balance of power.

According to Dorothy Smith, for example, 'Though women's participation in the educational process at all levels has increased this century it remains within marked boundaries' the most important of which is 'that which reserves to men control of the policy-making and decision-making apparatus in the education system.' (Smith, 1978, p. 287.) Dale Spender even argues that women might comprise 50 per cent of educational policy and decision makers and still have very little power. After all, she points out, 'women comprise 51 per cent of the population and are without power. It is erroneous to assume that there is a one-to-one relationship between women and men in a society predicated on sexual inequality.' (Spender, 1981, p. 113.)

Third, radical feminists reject the argument that it is women's own attitudes which are now the major obstacle to their further advancement. They pour scorn on the 'fashionable' view that if women are given enough sympathetic and supportive advice about pursuing non-traditional degrees and careers they will begin to succeed in these traditionally male preserves. According to Dale Spender 'such superficial analyses and solutions are insulting to women'. In some respects 'non traditional areas' is a euphemism for 'bastions of male power' and to suggest that the problem consists of women's inability to recognize that the area is open to them rather than one of men protecting their power base, provides more insights about who generates explanations than it does about women.

Finally, radical feminists claim that not only is the decision making structure of all welfare institutions controlled by men to their own advantage but also that the knowledge on which welfare services are based, because it too is controlled by men, is inherently sexist. Thus even women doctors learn – and many accept – that women are by nature neurotic emotional creatures who cannot be trusted to make their own medical decisions nor to receive full information about their own bodies and illnesses. This particular radical critique of male dominated welfare has been most fully developed in relation to the male domination of academic knowledge and disciplines. Radical feminists insist that even academic subjects at which women traditionally succeed, such as history and English literature, are predominantly taught from works by men about men and thus teach women that 'they are not as worthy and do not count as much' as men. So called 'male' scientific subjects also encompass, according to radical feminists, a great deal of sexist ideology masquerading as scientific objectivity. According to Kathy Overfield, for example, men will only allow women to join their science if women accept their own inferiority, accept male scientists' sexist view of women's nature and learn to exploit the natural world as men do in a 'logical' and 'emotionless' way. Overfield therefore concludes that women should firmly reject any invitation from men to join scientific pursuits on men's terms. (Overfield, 1981.)

The radical conclusion reached by those feminists who interpret women's recent 'progress' in welfare institutions as no progress at all is that women should give up trying to persuade men to let them play an equal role in man-made institutions. The only way to liberate women from male domination and oppression is to set up separate women-only institutions.

Socialist feminists' critique of reformism

Socialist feminists are not so antagonistic as radical feminists but they do express certain doubts about a reformist strategy. First, socialist feminists do not accept that sex discrimination within welfare institutions is somehow accidental or inadvertent. They link the way in which women are treated by welfare institutions to the needs of capitalism. According to Rosemary Deem, for example,

> Since the 'real' place of women in capitalist societies is in the family, any careers advice which girls receive at school is likely to be limited in extent and frequently not taken seriously either by those offering it or those receiving it.   (Deem, 1978, p. 51)

Similarly, whereas the radical feminist Mary Daly talks about 'the medically masterminded maze of lethal "choices" among surgical, chemical and mechanical solutions to The Contraceptive Problem' (Daly, 1979, p. 239), Lesley Doyal, a socialist feminist, links family planning to the needs of capitalism:

> it is important to recognise that the extension of family planning (in the postwar period) was not just in the interests of individual women, but was at the same time in the interests of capitalism in a broader sense. Women became more easily available for paid work: the nuclear family was strengthened and 'problem families' which might have to be maintained by the state at great expense could be induced not to have any more children by the availability of free contraceptive supplies.
> (Doyal, 1979, p. 231)

Second, although socialist feminists accept that liberal feminist reformism can and does benefit white middle-class women they emphasize that social class and race are key variables in women's welfare experiences and stress that working-class and black women are far less likely than white middle-class women to benefit from equal opportunities programmes in the welfare field. For example, the proportion of female medical students may have risen significantly in recent years but female entrants to medical school are even more likely to be from a white upper- or middle-class background than their male counterparts.

Socialist feminists explain the discrepancy between the academic achievements of girls from different social classes partly in relation to the demands of capitalism for a continuing supply of cheap manual labour.

According to Rosemary Deem:

The more academically successful, middle-class schoolgirls are less likely to experience sexism in careers advice than are working-class girls since there is some provision for the former to enter the labour market in a serious way. Working-class girls, on the other hand, may be channelled into a narrow avenue of unskilled or temporary work.   (Deem, 1978, p. 51)

Socialist feminists have also emphasized the different types of social control exercised by the medical profession over women from different classes and races. While some doctors may try to push middle-class women into mothering they may simultaneously be forcibly sterilizing poor or black women. In order to combat these very different types of oppression, socialists argue, it is essential that feminists understand and apply a theory of class conflict as well as feminist theories of patriarchy to their analysis of women's experience of welfare services.

Finally, socialist feminist analyses of women's experiences of health care emphasize the links between profit making industries and the NHS. Doyal, for example, agrees with liberal feminists that doctors have been encouraged by their own upbringing and by their sexist medical education to assume that their women patients are 'neurotic' but she goes on to emphasize the key role which drug companies play in encouraging doctors to over-treat women with highly profitable tranquillizers and anti-depressants. Doyal also argues that interventionist techniques in obstetrics which deny women any control over their own labour have been encouraged by the medical equipment manufacturers for whom obstetrics has become a profitable growth area (Doyal, 1979, chapter 6).

Although socialist feminists do not believe that the replacement of capitalism by socialism would by itself remove all forms of sex discrimination from welfare institutions, which have traditionally benefited certain individual men as well as capitalism, they do claim that socialism informed by feminism is the only ultimate answer to the double oppression experienced by working class women within the existing welfare system.

Conclusion

It is notoriously difficult to evaluate the impact of any social movement including feminism. Even if changes have occurred in welfare institutions in the last twenty years which appear to go some way towards meeting feminists' demands, it is by no means certain that such changes are the direct result of feminist actions. For example, the Engineering Council's strong and active support for the 1984 'Women Into Science and Technology' campaign may, at first sight, appear to be a major coup for the EOC. On closer analysis, however, it is quite clear that the Engineering Council's main concern is to remedy a severe shortage of first class professional engineers, technicians and craftsmen. As Sue Onians succinctly puts it 'Industry is beginning to realise that women could fill its skills gap.' (Onians, 1983, p. 14.) Optimistic feminists might interrupt here to ask 'What does it matter why change occurs as long as it benefits women?' History suggests, however, that feminists ignore at their peril the motives which lie behind men's apparent conversion to feminist causes. The history of women's fight to enter the medical profession demonstrates that women have been allowed into the medical profession at times of an acute shortage of doctors such as during the First and Second World Wars, only to be excluded again once the shortage of men has passed. In 1984 one regional health authority in Britain announced that it was planning to abolish part-time medical jobs. Dr Paul Walker defending the cuts argued that it was a 'logical man's approach' to abolish part-time training posts rather than have posts cut across the board. The authority originally introduced the part-time posts to meet the needs of newly qualified women doctors. But in future Dr Walker admitted married women would have to compete with men for the same posts. 'I would agree,' he concluded, 'that an appointing committee, faced with a man who could do sessions totalling ten hours and a woman who could do only six are likely to choose the former.' (Walker, 1984.) Women currently being lured into a career in engineering might wish to take particular note of this withdrawal of support to married women doctors now that – once again – an acute shortage of doctors has been transformed into a surfeit.

A second problem in attempting to interpret the evidence on women's progress in welfare institutions is that sexism and sex discrimination are not always overt and thus relatively easy to identify and attack. Since covert discrimination is, by its very nature, difficult to identify, it is particularly difficult to assess just how extensive it still is and exactly what effects it is having on those female welfare clients who continue to experience it.

A third problem is that of assessing how much time should be allowed to elapse before pronouncing judgment on a particular reform. Liberal reformist feminists claim that women must be patient. They should accept, for example, that changes in educational practice will take many years to improve girls' ultimate educational achievements. Critics of feminist reformism on the other hand do not accept that lack of time is the main explanation for the continuing existence of sexual inequalities in the educational field or elsewhere.

The many problems inherent in any attempt to interpret the empirical evidence on women's changing welfare experiences pale into insignificance beside the difficulties involved in evaluating the different interpretations put on this evidence by the various strands of feminism.

Liberal feminists claim at least a limited success for their reformist strategies, largely because they are not seeking to achieve anything more than limited reforms of existing society. Their main aim has been to secure equal opportunities for individual women with individual men. They have fought for individual female welfare professionals to enjoy equal career opportunities with their male colleagues. They have not sought to erase all job differentials within welfare institutions in order to eliminate all sex/class inequalities. Nor have they sought to seize power from the men who control welfare institutions in order to re-create these services according to radically different principles and values. The argument that the fields in which some women are achieving greater success – such as the scientific disciplines – are based on male values and therefore not worthy of female participation cuts very little ice with most liberal feminists.

Radical feminists on the other hand regard such liberal reforms as tokenism and demand that the very nature of welfare institutions be transformed, a transformation which most radical feminists believe will not take place without a revolutionary struggle. Similarly, socialist feminists will not be contented with significant gains for middle-class women which do nothing to alter the oppressed position of working-class women under capitalism. Socialist feminists insist, too, that women's oppression cannot be significantly transformed until revolutionary changes have been achieved. The main criticism levelled against liberal feminists by both radical and socialist feminists is not that reformist strategies are totally useless but that liberal feminists' goals are too narrow. However, it is quite logical to argue that the goals of liberal feminism are not radical enough but still to continue to support campaigns for limited welfare gains for women whilst waiting for more radical changes to society as a whole. Indeed, this is just the strategy advocated by Zillah Eisenstein. A strong critic of the limited vision of liberal feminism, Eisenstein, nevertheless, urges all feminists to push the State 'as far as it can go toward the equality of opportunity of women'. By doing this, she claims, feminists will make some real gains for women. More significantly they will learn that the patriarchal state 'cannot abide women's actual equality with men. As feminists uncover this reality for themselves in their struggles with the state, they will begin to build a feminist politics that moves beyond liberalism.' (Eisenstein, 1981, p. 222.)

In other words, by supporting liberal strategies for reform more radical feminists will prepare the way for the revolutionary struggle which must take place if women are ever to gain full equality with men.

If, as Eisenstein claims, reformist struggles for limited gains for women are the starting point for a feminist revolution, why have so many feminists apparently now abandoned the fight to reform mainstream welfare institutions? Partly perhaps because in recent years this fight has become so dispiriting. The reaction of some feminists to the severe cuts in welfare services and the intransigence displayed by the Conservative Government against virtually all feminist demands for better welfare services for women has been to retreat from political campaigning into the relative safety of personal politics and alternative lifestyles. Denise Riley suggests, for example, that the feminist goal of sharing child care equally between fathers and mothers may be a perfectly valid goal in its own right but that it is in danger of being adopted as a substitute for continuing the political, public battle for nurseries, play centres, school meals, and a better level of child benefit (Riley, 1983b). Whilst fully understanding and sympathizing with feminists' despairing retreat from conventional political campaigning, the authors believe that it is essential for all feminists to struggle against the superficially attractive option of critical aloofness from 'reformist' struggles. It may be exciting to argue that existing welfare services are appalling, oppressive, patriarchal institutions. It may be less exciting to tease out real improvements in women's experiences of mainstream welfare institutions and services. *Spare Rib* is much more entertaining than EOC documents which cautiously describe slow progress towards a much less overtly sexist education system. Yet these rather dull signs of progressive activity are ignored at women's peril. Empirical evidence carefully collected by feminist reformers strongly suggests that hard work and constant pressure can result in some welfare gains for at least some women.

The task of reforming mainstream welfare institutions is undoubtedly an uphill one, but that task is made infinitely more difficult if the feminist movement withdraws its support and simply keeps its principles pure by sniping at oppressive forms of welfare from a safe distance. If women's existing welfare experiences are still too frequently negative and oppressive feminists must surely keep fighting for reforms to existing welfare institutions however dispirited they become when met by both overt and covert resistance from those with the power to determine welfare policies and practices.

9

Separatist strategies for change

While some feminists have concentrated on changing mainstream welfare institutions from within, others have challenged the welfare system from without by creating and sustaining alternative, separatist, welfare services. The key characteristics of these services – at least in theory – are that they are run exclusively by women for women according to the feminist principles of co-operation and liberation. We can identify three main objectives of this separatist strategy: first, to provide non-sexist alternative welfare services to women who would otherwise have no choice but to use sexist, controlling forms of welfare, or perhaps receive no service at all; second, to challenge mainstream welfare institutions by giving women as much knowledge as possible about their own welfare needs and potential ways of meeting them; third, to develop a new relationship between welfare providers and clients, based on shared knowledge and power within non-hierarchical, democratic welfare structures, which could again challenge conventional, hierarchical welfare institutions.

Separatist welfare services for women such as women's study courses which have been set up outside mainstream educational institutions, rape crisis centres, women only health centres and Women's Aid's network of refuges for battered women are examples of what some feminists call 'prefigurative struggles'. In this particular context, 'prefigurative' means the creation of alternative welfare services intended to provide role models or practice runs for an eventual revolutionary transformation of mainstream welfare institutions. In this chapter we will describe and evaluate just two of these prefigurative feminist alternatives, feminist health care services provided by the Women's Health Movement and feminist run refuges for battered women. We have chosen these two developments rather than, for example, women-only study courses, because they have been such an important focus for the separatist movement and because we now have enough empirical evidence to attempt to evaluate their significance.

The American women's health movement

The evidence presented in this section will be based on the American women's health movement because British feminists have not developed separatist strategies to the same extent and therefore the clearest model we have of a prefigurative separatist feminist health care system is an American one.

The women's health movement grew out of the WLM's struggle to reform the American abortion laws and also developed from women's experiences in consciousness raising groups. Feminist activists fighting for better conventional health care services for women, such as abortion on demand, soon realized that in order to achieve liberation women needed much more than simply more of the same type of male dominated medical care. In consciousness raising groups thousands of women shared their health worries and negative experiences of health care services and discovered that their own problems were not unique but were part of a general medical oppression of female patients. Women began to share negative feelings about their own bodies and sexuality and discovered that the treatment they received from doctors reinforced, or even created, these negative feelings. Feminists began to realize that they needed to explore their own bodies in order to build up shared, positive knowledge about being female. This sharing began informally in small groups, but by the early 1970s a women's health movement had emerged and by 1975 there were over 1000 groups in the United States which identified themselves as part of a diffuse but nevertheless influential movement. During the early 1970s women's health groups also began to spring up in Britain and other western countries.

These groups have produced a great deal of health care literature including perhaps the best known feminist health care book, *Our Bodies Ourselves*. This literature is quite different from

157

traditional health education material. Rather than stressing that self-care is merely a first step before seeking expert professional medical advice, it emphasizes that women themselves are the experts in relation to their own bodies and health care needs; that they should be proud of their bodies and that they can learn to identify and treat many of the so-called 'minor' women's problems which have received such poor attention from the medical profession.

The women's health movement has also encouraged groups of women to help each other through practical exercises such as examining their own cervixes. These exercises were originally intended to build up women's confidence and pride in their own bodies. Some groups however moved beyond simply learning about their own bodies and began to identify and treat a range of women's problems from thrush to missed periods. According to Ruzek: 'the "invention" of self-help gynaecology more than any other event transformed health and body issues into a separate social movement.' (Ruzek, 1978, p. 53.) Ruzek claims that self-examination and self-help gynaecology were 'revolutionary concepts' since they provided women with the opportunity 'to reclaim parts of themselves controlled by male professionals.' By 1972 Carol Downes, one of the original founders of the self-help radical approach to women's health care problems, was publicly declaring that ordinary women could quite easily perform a whole range of 'medical' techniques:

> Abortions are so simple they are downright dull; vaginal infections are diagnosed with a microscope; pap smears are easier to do than setting our hair; fitting a diaphragm is less complicated than stuffing a turkey. We can do these things. (quoted by Ruzek, 1978, p. 54.)

The medical profession was not prepared to accept this challenge to its authority without a fight. Doctors were particularly incensed at women's groups which practised menstrual extraction, a technique which was primarily a do-it-yourself early abortion. In September 1972 the feminist Women's Health Centre in Los Angeles was searched by police and Carol Downes and Coleen Wilson were arrested on charges of practising medicine without a licence. Downes elected to stand trial and this trial became a *cause célèbre* within the American women's movement. Downes was finally acquitted but after the trial Jeanne Hirsch commented:

What man would be put under police surveillance for six
months for looking at his penis? What man would have to
spend $20,000 and two months in court for looking at the penis
of his brother? This case is a clear cut version of the position
of women in America – the lengths to which we must go and
obstacles which must be overcome to be FREE. (Ruzek, 1978,
p. 58.)

During the early 1970s a number of feminist health clinics or
centres opened up throughout the United States. Ruzek has
distinguished two main types of clinic which she labels traditional
feminist and radical feminist. Traditional feminist clinics are run
by female paraprofessionals and trained volunteers who provide
much of the care and attempt to minimize the status and power
differentials between health care providers and health care users.
Female doctors are employed or volunteer to work in these clinics
but they are only called in to deal with more complex cases and
to provide those services, such as prescribing, which the other
staff are not qualified or allowed to do. Women patients are
encouraged to talk for as long as they wish about their worries
and problems and one of the main objectives of workers in these
clinics is to share as much medical knowledge as possible with the
patients. At this point readers accustomed to the professionally
dominated patriarchal type of health care delivery which typifies
mainstream medical services may wonder what is 'traditional'
about such clinics, but according to Ruzek such clinics have been
criticized by some feminists because although they may change
professional behaviour and practices they do not challenge the key
assumption that welfare professionals should continue to define
patients' health care needs and provide routine services for them.
  In radical feminist health care settings much greater emphasis is
placed on encouraging women to assume primary responsibility
for their own health care by defining their own health care needs
and by learning to perform basic health services for themselves.
Doctors are called upon only as a last resort, once women
themselves have decided what treatment they need. The most
important underlying principle of radical feminist health care
settings is that laywomen control everything that happens within
them and thus 're-establish their right and responsibility to
manage normal life-events which they do not regard as medical
affairs'. In radical feminist settings medical authority has no more
status than women's personal experiences and the imbalance of
power between welfare professionals and their clients is thus
reduced to a minimum.

Even the most radical feminist clinics have attracted a number of criticisms from some sceptical feminists. First, most feminist clinics have concentrated on a small range of health care services and techniques and some feminists have suggested that they simply perform the type of tasks which most doctors do not want to do anyway, leaving men to monopolize the more prestigious areas of medicine. Not only does this mean that women still have to rely on conventional medical services for more complicated forms of health care but it may also lead to female health care professionals – particularly active feminists – being channelled into low paid, low status work in feminist clinics. Ultimately, an all-female ghetto of low status medical practice may be created. In response, radical feminists argue that continuing to work with men drains feminists' energies and subverts their radical goals. Mary Howell has even suggested that feminists should found their own medical school which would produce explicitly feminist health care professionals, who would then work exclusively in health care services run for women by women. (Howell, 1975, p. 50.)

Second, some concern has been expressed over the standards and safety records of certain alternative health care techniques such as menstrual extraction. In reply, radical feminist health workers point out that the safety record of many of the conventional medical treatments women undergo is appalling. Third, socialist feminists in particular have suggested that the existence of feminist medical services and the very considerable efforts needed to create and sustain them may distract feminists' energies from more fundamental campaigns against those factors which cause women's health problems in the first place. Whereas radical feminists have stressed the biological dimensions of women's health problems and have therefore given priority to the creation of health care services which will ultimately give women complete control over their own reproduction, socialist feminists have stressed social and economic factors as causes of women's ill health and have been less enthusiastic about the liberating potential of separatist health care systems. According to Doyal, for example, waged work and domestic labour can both be hazardous to women's health and feminists must therefore struggle not only 'for non-sexist and appropriate medical care, but also for a broader social and economic transformation leading to healthier living and working conditions for both women and men'. (Doyal, 1983, p. 30.)

Feminist health care in Britain

In October 1973, Carol Downes visited Britain and gave a series of talks explaining feminist self-care techniques and practices. Following her visit a number of British women's health groups were set up, and British feminists began to arm themselves with feminist knowledge about their own bodies and about their own health care needs and experiences. From the start, however, many members of these groups dismissed the idea of setting up full-time feminist women's health centres and clinics along the American model. There appear to be two key factors behind the British WLM's lack of interest in establishing major alternatives to mainstream medical care services. First, the existence of a free universal health care system – despite many women's negative experiences of it – strongly militates against the viability of any alternative services. Either radical alternative proposals must attract sufficient funding to be able to provide a free service to all their potential clients – and it is highly unlikely that such funds will be forthcoming at a time when the NHS itself is so short of resources – or alternative services must charge clients who wish to use them. Most British feminists are strongly opposed to all forms of private medicine and do not wish to set up any services which would be available only to relatively well-off women.

The second main reason why radical feminist health care alternatives have not developed in Britain is that socialist feminists have played a much more significant role in the British WLM than in America, where radical feminists have been much more powerful. British socialist feminists emphasize the importance of campaigning to improve health care services for women within the NHS. Faced with attacks on welfare spending, which have increased dramatically since 1979, feminist health activists in Britain have given priority to defending the NHS and in particular the many essential services which it provides for women. They have also supported female health care workers in their fights to protect their own jobs. Since 1979 women's health groups have linked up with female health workers to fight for such causes as the continued existence of the Elizabeth Garret Anderson hospital which Norman Fowler has tried to close on the grounds that it is an 'unnecessary luxury'.

Jill Rakusen, whilst accepting that the NHS clearly needs to be vigorously defended against right wing ideological and economic attacks, has suggested that British feminists have tended to be too uncritical in their demands for more NHS services to meet women's health care needs. She argues that when feminists uncritically demand 'more' or 'better' ante-natal care within the NHS they may be in danger of both reinforcing an unnecessarily medicalized approach to childbirth and obscuring the real causes of peri-natal mortality such as poverty and environment. Rakusen therefore urges all feminists to support and encourage alternative feminist health care initiatives without giving up the struggle to defend and improve the NHS itself. 'What kind of NHS are we ever going to have' she asks 'unless it is going to learn from developments and pioneering which can rarely, if ever, be initiated within it?' (Rakusen, 1982, p. 21.)

One innovative and separatist development which has taken place within the NHS has been the creation of Well Women Clinics. The campaign for Well Women Clinics began in Islington, London when a group of women from Islington Trades Council and the National Abortion Campaign joined forces with the local Community Health Council and succeeded in establishing five Well Women Clinics, once weekly, in Islington health centres. Since then Well Women Clinics have been set up in a number of towns and cities throughout Britain although the struggle to establish more Well Women Clinics is meeting with resistance from male dominated NHS decision making bodies in several areas. The main aims and objectives of Well Women Clinics as set out in a National Guidelines document drawn up by the National Association of CHCs are:

to provide a service specifically for women which meets all their health care needs;
to provide this comprehensive service in a relaxed and friendly atmosphere;
to provide an accessible service available to all women;
to provide a service run for women by women. (Manchester's Community Health Councils, p. 2).

Despite this objective of providing a 'comprehensive service', existing Well Women Clinics do *not* actually treat the women who attend them at all. If any problems which need to be treated are detected the clinic's staff will discuss them fully with the woman concerned but they will then have no alternative but to refer her back to her own GP for treatment or, if her GP agrees, to refer her directly to a consultant or other specialist service. Feminist defenders of the existing model of Well Women Clinics point out, however, that the lack of conventional medical treatment in these centres is an advantage rather than a restriction since it prevents them from becoming too similar to conventional health centres. It ensures that the main services provided in Well Women Clinics are listening to women and giving them potentially liberating information about themselves and their health care needs.

Well Women Clinics are usually staffed by all female health care teams comprising a mix of health visitors, counsellors, community health workers, nurses, doctors and possibly social workers. Volunteers may help to run the centres and may provide very limited services to clients but they are usually accepted only as adjuncts to a professional medical team. A proposal for Well Women Clinics in Manchester stated firmly:

> the provision of all the basic medical and counselling services must be provided by paid employees of the NHS or Local Authority. No service offered should be dependent on voluntary help. This is often unreliable and usually takes more time to organise than the help it provides. (Manchester's Community Health Councils, 1981, p. 10.)

Those campaigning for Well Women Clinics emphasize that staff should work as a team and that doctors will simply be members of that team rather than being in charge. Nevertheless, the role of doctors in Well Women Clinics appears to be a central one. The Manchester proposals even suggest that a doctor might lead discussions of health issues by women in groups and contribute medical advice to the establishment and running of self-help groups, a far cry from the type of women's self-help health groups envisaged by radical feminists!

British Well Women Clinics do place some emphasis on encouraging women to form self-help groups and on promoting health knowledge and awareness among lay women but the primary aim of such education appears to be to prevent ill health and to encourage limited mutual support amongst groups of dieters, smokers and women suffering from certain types of disease. The Manchester proposals for Well Women Clinics do not suggest that lay women should be encouraged to treat themselves in order to reduce their dependency on the medical profession. On the contrary, one of the key objectives of British Well Women Clinics is to attract into the mainstream health care system women who would 'normally stay away from doctors for reasons of class, culture or because they are intimidated by male GP's.' (Manchester's Community Health Councils, 1981, p. 4.)

The main criticism which can be levelled at those Well Women

Clinics which have been established within the NHS is that they
do little, if anything, to transfer significant powers from the
medical profession to women themselves. In some instances Well
Women Clinics may actually increase the amount of medical
control exercised over women's lives, for example by teaching
women that they ought to have regular screening for breast and
cervical cancer. Many British feminists have supported campaigns
for improved screening services for women but some American
radical feminist health campaigners are not only extremely
sceptical of the benefits of such screening but may also regard its
imposition on 'well' women as just another example of negative
medical control (see Mary Daly). Women who have attended
Well Women Clinics, however, regard them in a very positive
light. The fact that the two clinics which were established in
South Manchester in the early 1980s have been so overwhelmed
by patient demand that they have had to refuse to accept any
women living outside small catchment areas speaks for itself. One
satisfied client has summed up the differences between her
experiences at a Well Women Clinic and her previous medical
experiences as follows:

> Oh, it was very different. It was very friendly and very warm
> and responsive. People were very interested in you as a person
> rather than you as a medical condition, and to work out your
> medical problems as part of your whole life-style. I think that's
> important and also they were all women doctors, nurses and
> helpers. You get doctors coming round acting almost as
> receptionists to see that you're all right and there doesn't seem
> to be the sort of hierarchical structure that you get in hospitals
> and clinics. (Manchester Community Health Councils 1981,
> Appendix IV.)

Client satisfaction is not the only indication that Well Women
Clinics are not simply more of the same, negative, controlling
type of medical care. Whilst some proposals for Well Women
Clinics can be interpreted as being based on a conventional model
of health care provision which is to be changed only in style
rather than substance, they nevertheless contain some more
radical objectives. The CHCs' national guidelines, for example,
state that the clinic staff should be careful not to make
assumptions about women's sexuality, whether heterosexual,
homosexual or bisexual, and that staff should be aware that
lesbian women may want children and should be able to advise
them about artificial insemination. The emphasis in Well Women

Clinics on communication and shared knowledge is certainly an advance on traditional authoritarian styles of health care. For example, Judith Gray, one of the doctors who helped to set up a clinic in Manchester stated: 'We think that education and knowing more about our own bodies is a really important part in taking control over our own health.' (Manchester Community Health Councils 1981, Appendix IV.) Well Women Clinics do not, at present, seriously threaten mainstream conventional medical practices and if they did develop along even more radical lines they might well face strong and concerted opposition from the majority of the medical profession. Nevertheless, Well Women Clinics do provide both female health care workers and female patients with an alternative model of primary health care and it is possible that this first chink in the defensive armoury of mainstream medical practice will create further demands from both female health care providers and female clients for changes within the NHS.

Women's aid

In 1972 Erin Pizzey set up the first refuge for battered women in Chiswick and succeeded in attracting considerable media coverage. Thereafter, women throughout the country began to form groups and set up refuges. In 1974, twenty-seven of these groups joined together in a national conference and formed the National Women's Aid Federation. At the next national conference, in 1975, Erin Pizzey left after a row and has gone her own way ever since, but the Women's Aid Federation has gone on growing. By 1980 it comprised ninety-nine groups running approximately 200 refuges. The Women's Aid Federation is a non-hierarchical organization, with explicitly feminist aims and objectives.

In 1981, the report of a national survey of refuges belonging to the Women's Aid Federation set out the key principles of these refuges as follows:

they accept women into their refuges on the women's own definition of need and women can stay as long as they need to re-organise their lives. Residents organise the day-to-day running of the house. Mutual self-help is stressed as an important step towards women gaining self-confidence and being able to cope when they leave the refuge. The Women's

Aid group is there to provide whatever information and assistance women need, as far as resources allow. Groups also aim to publicise their work giving talks and presenting exhibitions to increase public awareness of battering. (Binney, Harkell and Nixon, 1981, p. 23.)

Jan Pahl's study of the Canterbury women's refuge summarized the key principles of the women who established it as 'self-help, mutual support, power sharing' and an 'open-door policy' (Pahl, 1978, p. 5).

We can see from these statements that in theory at least feminist run refuges are based on principles which vary significantly from those which underlie statutory, professionally or bureaucratically run welfare services. Statutory welfare services still expect the client to hand themselves over to the expert and passively to accept help and advice rather than to participate in the decision making process. Clients of statutory welfare services are usually treated as individuals and therefore have little opportunity to provide each other with mutual support. Faced with severe resource restraints, statutory welfare agencies invariably ration their services – in theory, at least, giving priority to those in greater need. Clients themselves play an insignificant part in this rationing process. Before the existence of women's refuges local authorities frequently refused to recognize that battered women had genuine housing needs and simply urged them to go home and make it up with their violent partners. Battered women who were accepted by local authorities as homeless were likely to be accommodated in the notorious 'Part III hostels'. Ironically, the punitive deterrent rules governing access to this accommodation for homeless families, which included denying husbands and wives the right to stay together, inadvertently gave battered women living in these hostels some protection from their violent partners.

One can envisage that if the State were to set up a network of statutory refuges for battered women, staffed by trained social workers, women seeking a place would have to produce firm evidence proving that they were genuinely battered. Their own definition of their need would not be recognized as sufficient grounds for admission and waiting lists for places or a points system prioritizing needs might even be established. A new professional skill – that of judging how battered a particular woman was – would soon be added to the range of social workers' professional expertise and powers.

There is clearly a wide gap between feminist principles and

feminist welfare provision and the principles and practices of statutory welfare agencies. But we cannot judge Women's Aid refuges solely on their principles. There is often a gap between the stated objectives of a welfare agency and what it actually does in practice. We must therefore examine the limited evidence that exists on how far the feminist principles behind the setting up of women's refuges have survived the many practical problems faced by any voluntary welfare service.

Many of the women interviewed for the national survey of women's refuges had been encouraged to deal with statutory agencies themselves, in order to gain experience and self-confidence. A number of these women clearly benefited from the self-help philosophy of the refuges and gained in confidence by doing things for themselves. Women interviewed by Jan Pahl often commented that their stay in the refuge had made them feel 'more self-confident, more independent and more determined'. (Pahl, 1978, p. 53.) Not all the women, however, appreciated the efforts made by the support group to encourage women to do things for themselves rather than do everything for them. One woman who told Jan Pahl that she had hated the time she spent in the refuge, commented 'it does make women more independent because there is so little support'. (Pahl, 1978, p. 54.) The fact that some did not like being pushed to be independent is not in itself evidence against the putting into practice of feminist principles within welfare institutions. Anyone who has learnt to be totally dependent on welfare professionals, who is tied to being a passive client or who has simply learned the helpless dependency which appears to be a feature of some battered women's lives will clearly find the process of learning to be independent a difficult and sometimes painful one. The evidence that in most refuges women are encouraged to help themselves – however painful that may be at first – is a sign that the feminist principle of encouraging women to be autonomous is being put into practice through the refuge system.

Women can gain strengths not only from helping themselves but also by helping others in a similar position to themselves and from receiving support from them. Evidence from women who have stayed in refuges suggests that despite poor physical conditions and overcrowding which make co-operative living in refuges difficult and stressful, the women do give each other a great deal of mutual support. One woman summed up the benefits of this mutual support thus:

After two or three days when you've been there and you see

another woman come in you try to help her, like you've been helped. You can fit in and discuss things and you know that you're not the only person in the world that's been battered, or even gone through a bad time and it sort of helps you in that way. (Binney, Harkell and Nixon, 1981, p. 57.)

Power sharing has proved to be one of the more difficult principles to put into practice, partly because some of the workers themselves find it difficult to work in a role with little status or power but also because many of the refuges' clients and outside agencies tend to have considerable difficulties in coming to terms with welfare organizations where no one is 'in charge'.

Pahl concluded from her study of a refuge which lacked an authority figure during the first months of its existence that a majority of women would have liked there to be someone in charge, and there was also a demand 'for someone who would give more authoritative advice' (p. 54). Pahl suggests, however, that the need for someone in authority to enforce minimal standards to prevent a refuge from becoming too squalid does not negate the principles of client self-help, autonomy and power sharing which lay behind the initial lack of authority figure. Moreover, Pahl points out that a minority of the women emphasized the advantage of a non-hierarchical egalitarian structure. One woman commented: 'This is an institution run by women for women, therefore there should be a complete equal say for everybody.' (Pahl, 1978, p. 55.)

Refuges run on radical lines not only have to face resistance from some clients, they also face initial misapprehension and even hostility from many of the outside bodies with which they come into contact. Sophie Watson, who worked in a refuge for eighteen months, found that statutory social service workers were often reluctant to deal directly with the battered women themselves and made it clear that they would have preferred to deal with the workers rather than the women, thus maintaining 'professional distance and the power of the expert'. (Watson, 1983, p. 97.) Again, however, whilst recognizing that a major problem faced by Women's Aid refuges is the pressing need for support from outside agencies, evidence that outside organizations sometimes find the lack of 'someone in charge' difficult to accept is not in itself a criticism of the way the refuges are run. Rather, it represents an important example of the difficulties which must be faced by any radically organized institution situated in a conservative society.

Most refuges have managed to sustain the principle of an open door policy despite very heavy demands on their severely limited space and resources. However, this policy has led to a severe problem of overcrowding in many refuges and the majority of the women living in them have experienced strong dissatisfaction with the physical conditions in which they and their children have to live. In some cases this has apparently contributed to some women staying only briefly in a refuge before returning home to a violent man. However, the problems of overcrowding and squalor are as much the result of chronic under-financing and lack of financial support from local authorities as they are of any open-door policies.

So far the small amount of empirical evidence on Women's Aid refuges which we have reviewed suggests that in the main the key feminist principles which lie behind the setting up of these refuges have been adhered to, despite the many severe problems faced by both the workers and the women themselves in putting these principles into practice. We must be careful, however, not to paint a picture of refuges as a totally successful example of feminist principles being translated into welfare practice.

One major criticism of Women's Aid refuges is that however radical their principles, in practice they mainly function to provide a much needed welfare service on the cheap. Local authorities and a range of statutory welfare services now make use of refuges and refer women in need on to them, but as yet the State has not provided regular substantial funding for Women's Aid. Consequently, not only are most refuges very short of basic facilities but also those who work in refuges are usually not well paid and have little job security. It is important to recognize, however, that refuges are in a dilemma. The more state funding feminist run refuges attract the more likely they are to have certain conditions imposed upon them by state officials – such as restricting the number living in the refuge at any one time, which may undermine the implementation of radical feminist principles.

A second criticism of Women's Aid is that it has not lived up to its own commitment to changing society's attitudes towards violence against women and thus tackling the problem at source rather than simply providing refuges to help the victims of this problem. One of the declared objectives of the Women's Aid Federation is:

> To educate and inform the public, the media, the police, the courts, the social services and other authorities with respect to the battering of women, mindful of the fact that this is the

result of the general position of women in society. (National Women's Aid Federation, 1980, p. 8.)

In 1980, the Women's Aid Federation claimed that the increasing numbers of enquiries they were receiving showed that they had had success in promoting awareness and understanding of the needs of battered women (NWAF Annual Report, 1979–80, p. 53). On the other hand, the Federation admitted that the workers in their national office had been so overwhelmed with administrative work within the Federation that they had been able to do less outward-looking education and publicity than they would have wished. Feminists involved in the Women's Aid Federation are particularly concerned to propagate an understanding of 'wife battering' based on theories of male power and female subordination in our society, yet the media has, on the whole, paid more attention to the views of Erin Pizzey who suggests that certain women attract violence and have a pathological need for it. Clearly by itself the Women's Aid Federation is not, however much time and energy its busy members manage to devote to campaigning, going to alter radically the overall position of women in society nor stop all male violence against women. The existence of refuges has at least drawn other welfare agencies' attention to the problem of violence against women in the home and social workers faced with a battered woman may now suggest that she contacts a refuge if one exists in her area.

It was largely due to the persistent campaigning by Women's Aid, supported by feminist lawyers and Jo Richardson, MP, that the Domestic Violence Act (1976) gave women the right to exclude a violent spouse from the joint home by use of an injunction and that the Housing (Homeless Persons) Act 1977 defined as unintentionally homeless women whose partners were likely to carry out a threat of violence against them. In theory this clause gave battered women a right to be rehoused. In practice, many battered women have been caught between these two Acts. Some housing authorities have insisted that rather than be rehoused women must obtain an injunction to evict their violent partners from their joint home. Yet such injunctions are difficult to obtain and even more difficult to enforce (see Wilson, 1983). Despite these very real practical weaknesses, however, we should not belittle the influence which Women's Aid has exerted over the state's policies towards the victims of marital violence. We should also emphasize that whilst Women's Aid has clearly not revolutionized most men's or women's attitudes towards women's subordinate position in the home, the very existence of refuges has enabled some battered women to become more independent. This in turn may have enabled them to gain greater self-esteem and thus to begin to see their own problems and subordinate position in a new and liberating way.

In the early 1980s, the outlook for Women's Aid refuges does not look at all secure. In 1981 the Federation reported that because of poor funding some groups had had to close down whilst others had had to make workers redundant. What funding there was from the Manpower Services Commission and Urban Aid was beginning to dry up and the local authorities were failing to take over funding on a permanent basis as Women's Aid groups had hoped. Despite these practical setbacks, however, we would maintain that the refuges set up by the groups affiliated to the Women's Aid Federation have provided a significant example of feminist welfare principles in practice. Not only have these refuges provided non-controlling, non-hierarchical support for women in desperate need, who previously had nowhere at all to go, but they have also become places 'where workers and women raise their own and others' political consciousness and go some way towards challenging capitalist and patriarchal social relations.' (Watson, 1983, p. 98.)

Conclusion

Only a tiny minority of women ever gain access to separatist feminist welfare services. Even in the United States where the self-help feminist health care movement achieved greatest momentum and publicity the great majority of women, especially working-class and black women do not use alternative health care services. Given the extreme difficulties of funding radical welfare innovations of any kind – particularly in Britain where the State does at least provide free universal health care and education to all its citizens – it is highly unlikely that separatist feminist welfare services will ever develop into anything more than very small scale alternatives to the statutory welfare services. In quantitative terms, therefore, feminist alternatives will never pose any major threat to the male dominated, professionally orientated mainstream welfare system.

Nevertheless, despite the severe problems faced by any group attempting to sustain non-statutory welfare services and despite the very small scale nature of existing feminist welfare services, we believe that feminists should continue to put at least some of their efforts into creating and developing alternative forms of welfare provision. We would suggest that the key significance of these small scale services lies in their potential as working models of egalitarian, liberating forms of welfare provision. Even the most committed feminists working in statutory welfare agencies are caught up in a tight web of unequal relationships. Not only do they face considerable restrictions and control from their superiors or employers, they also cannot escape the status and power gap between themselves and welfare clients. It is only when feminists set up and work within non-hierarchical welfare institutions that they are free to work out completely new, more equal relationships between themselves and welfare recipients. Even if only a very small proportion of feminist welfare workers and female clients experience these liberating welfare structures they can nevertheless provide inspiration for all those women still caught within the restraints of mainstream welfare institutions.

10

Conclusion

Throughout this book, we have compared and contrasted the
different approaches within feminism to the analysis of women's
position in society and how to change it. In this final chapter we
shall attempt to evaluate the potential of different feminist
strategies for changing the Welfare State in ways which will
significantly benefit women. As in chapters 7 and 9 we shall classify
these strategies as liberal/reformist, separatist and socialist feminist.

The main strength of liberal/reformist feminist campaigns for
equal rights and anti-discrimination laws and practices is that
such moderate – some might say minimal – demands do have
some chance of being taken up and implemented by politicians
and welfare managers who may not be at all responsive to more
radical feminist demands. Even small changes in mainstream
welfare services will affect large numbers of women. If state
secondary schools become just a little less overtly sexist, for
example, the great majority of girls will benefit albeit only
marginally. We cannot accept the extremist, cynical, view that *any*
improvements which take place in male dominated institutions or
in welfare organizations situated within a capitalist society are
worse than useless because they simply help to disguise women's
oppression and encourage women to accept their oppressed
position. We would rather have the very limited protection
offered by the Equal Pay and Sex Discrimination Acts than have
no equal rights legislation whatsoever.

Liberal feminists have also played an important role in widening
career opportunities for women. Whilst these cannot be said to

benefit the majority of women directly, liberal feminists would argue that they do so indirectly by, for example, widening the horizon of girls by presenting them with a wider range of role models.

A major weakness of the liberal/reformist feminists' approach to changing welfare services is that they tend seriously to underestimate the strength of those forces opposed to any major advances for women. These range from overt hostility on the part of some men to women entering currently male dominated areas, particularly at the higher levels of certain professions, to more subtle sexist biases in the structures and practices of social institutions. Furthermore, we do not believe that sexism alone accounts for women's oppression. At a time of cuts in the Welfare State, when houses are not being built and nurseries are being closed, it is all too clear that the Welfare State is limited by the constraints of capitalism. Economic ideologies can be just as devastating for women as sexist ideologies.

A second weakness of liberal/reformist feminist reforms, particularly where their emphasis is on career opportunities for women, is that they tend to be of most benefit to white, middle-class women. If women do eventually achieve equal results to men's in traditionally male academic disciplines it will still only be a tiny minority of women who will enjoy lucrative careers at the top of the scientific and technological professions. Recent changes in the rules governing social security benefits which have been designed to give more women claimants the same rights as men still leave many women struggling to bring up children on totally inadequate amounts of benefit. Campaigns to increase the proportion of women in medicine do little or nothing to attack the institutionalized racism which black women face when using the NHS. (See for example, Sheffield Black Women's Group 1984.)

A final criticism of liberal/reformist feminist strategies is that they are intended to reform rather than transform welfare institutions. They rely on welfare providers changing their behaviour towards women clients, and treating them in less sexist and controlling ways. Many feminists would argue that this approach can only make minor changes, since behaviour is not simply the result of goodwill or badwill, but is conditioned by the relationship between workers, and between workers and clients in hierarchical, professionalized organizations.

Radical and socialist feminists, including many who work within welfare institutions have developed a more sophisticated structural analysis of women's subordination. They have also begun to create explicitly feminist forms of welfare practice which take account of women's structural inequality. Their strategies for change are more radical than those of their liberal/reformist sisters and they do have some potential for helping even the most oppressed women in our society.

We are optimistic that increasing numbers of feminist and pro-feminist welfare professionals can – provided they receive strong support from a wider women's movement – develop ways of working with female welfare clients which will protect them from some of the more overt forms of sexism which are both intrinsic to state welfare institutions and which are imposed upon them by external pressures, in particular by the policies of a right-wing central government. We also believe that socialist and radical feminist welfare providers can create some opportunities, even within male dominated statutory welfare organizations, for working with female clients in liberating rather than merely protective ways. There are, however, limits to the possibility of creating pockets of feminist welfare practice within mainstream social services.

First, strongly committed feminist activists are still very thinly spread within the social services. Although women form the majority of basic grade social workers and teachers we must acknowledge that many of these women are not committed to feminism whilst some are overtly hostile to it. Nor can we assume that the increasing numbers of women doctors will inevitably improve the health care received by women patients. Too many women still report receiving sexist and patronizing advice from women doctors for us to assume that feminists have significantly challenged sexist professional ideologies.

This should not perhaps surprise us. When women enter traditionally male professions, they are faced with a barrage of institutional and cultural assumptions which embody the class, sexual and racial hierarchies of society. It requires a tremendous effort of courage and commitment to stand out against them.

Not all welfare professionals have the degree of autonomy over their work enjoyed by the medical professions. GPs have a contract with the NHS rather than being salaried employees slotted into a managerial hierarchy. The same is not true of social workers and teachers. Unsympathetic area team leaders or head teachers can threaten the careers and livelihoods of feminists who try to put their ideas into practice in the classroom, or in their work with clients. Feminists can, however, strengthen their position by joining together rather than struggling on in isolation. There are many examples of feminists working in particular welfare services forming groups both to give each other support and to develop collective strategies for change.

Conclusion

Feminist welfare providers can also fight against the individualization of women as welfare clients. Individual female clients do not always allow welfare professionals to reduce them to total passivity but at present many of the strategies open to them are the strategies of the powerless such as bursting into tears or using feminine charm to seduce male providers into giving them what they need. Feminist welfare providers can encourage women as clients to collectivize and to discuss their personal experiences of welfare within supportive groups. They can thus enable women to see their own strengths and to use those strengths collectively to fight for change within mainstream welfare organizations. More research on the forms of resistance already put up by both female welfare providers and clients against attempts to control and subordinate them could also reveal contradictions and areas of autonomy within all welfare institutions which those seeking change could further exploit.

Many feminist teachers and social workers are socialist feminists, and their feminism is not just a question of how they work with individual women or girls, but involves joining in wider campaigns to defend the Welfare State – in the trade union movement, and in a wide range of anti-cuts groups. They have attempted to inject into the traditional trade union and socialist preoccupations with jobs and the level of service, an awareness that the *quality* of the service and the social relations it embodies are of equal importance. This awareness has been associated with the development of new forms of struggle which challenge hierarchies as well as cuts and which attempt to link together the users of the services as well as providers. (See for example Cockburn; London Edinburgh Weekend Return Group.) Whilst feminists cannot claim to have been solely responsible for this reformulation of socialist thinking, it is probably true to say that, without the challenge posed by the women's movement, it would not have taken the direction it did.

The final strategy for change which we have explored is the creation of separatist women-only welfare services either within mainstream social services such as Well Women Clinics or as non-statutory services such as women's refuges run by Women's Aid. The key advantage of women only services which have been set-up outside the statutory framework is that they enable both welfare providers and welfare consumers to work together to create new forms of welfare provision based on the feminist principles of 'self help mutual support and power sharing'. They can thus provide not only practical help to their users but they may also enable some women to begin to challenge the dominant ideologies of their role, and to see their 'personal' problems as political issues. A battered woman entering a Women's Aid refuge receives, first and foremost, practical help and support. She may also come to realize, however, that violence against women is not just an individual problem but is related to women's position in society.

Of course, radical alternative welfare services of any kind face severe practical problems and limitations in the climate of the 1980s. They are kept chronically – sometimes acutely – short of resources and cannot therefore expand to meet more than a tiny fraction of the potential need they are intended to meet. Most women's refuges and most well women clinics are almost overwhelmed by the demand their existence has created. Practical problems are a severe limitation on the potential of separatist feminist welfare services but we must also consider the even more fundamental issue of the principle of providing a wide range of separatist services.

All feminists may accept the logic of separatist women-only welfare services which respond to needs which are peculiarly female. One does not have to be 'anti-men' to accept that self-help groups of women will have more sympathy for and understanding of gynaecological problems than male specialists. One does not have to be a radical feminist to support separatist rape-crisis centres, refuges for battered women and other women-only services for those who are the victims of male violence. We are, however, less happy about campaigns for separatist services to meet needs which women share to a great extent with men. There are three main reasons for our unease. First, separatist institutions such as women-only medical schools or universities run the danger of becoming second-class ghettoes, or rather of being labelled as such by men who could happily continue to dominate unchanged mainstream prestigious institutions. Second, many feminist goals can only be achieved if we break down the traditional sexual division of labour which reduces parenting to motherhood. This involves changing the role of men in our society as well as women, and it is difficult to envisage such change happening unless feminists can find space to work with men both individually and collectively. Third, many of the limits to the Welfare State stem from capitalism rather than patriarchy. Although welfare is less central to men's lives than women's, many men also experience poverty, unequal health care and poor housing. Although most men do not have to carry the burden of caring for dependants, we should not therefore assume that men are indifferent to the plight of their children or elderly parents. Past experience has shown the labour movement prepared to accommodate itself to capitalism at the expense of women. However, within the socialist movement there have always been men prepared to see that working-class interests include women as well as men.

An overall strategy

Both liberal, reformist and separatist approaches have their limits, although each also has its place in an overall strategy. Such a strategy should, we believe have three elements. First we need to ensure that all citizens enjoy basic political, and civil rights, ensuring equality of treatment for all regardless of sex. Equal pay and sex discrimination legislation *are* needed. It is scandalous that married women are still discriminated against in so many overt ways in the social security system. Despite the well-rehearsed arguments against legislation as an inadequate palliative, it is useful as a statement of intent within a broader strategy, and does offer some protection against the worst forms of exploitation. It would also help prevent the *withdrawal* of gains women have made.

Second, and more fundamentally, society must give greater priority to the caring role, by making more resources available for carers whether in the home or in statutory or non-statutory institutions, and by making paid work more flexible so that men or women can choose how they balance paid work and caring in the home. To some extent, such changes are against the interests of men. However, as unemployment undermines the patriarchal notion of the male breadwinner, and more mothers work outside the home, capitalism itself may be opening up spaces for women to persuade some men at least to consider such changes.

Turning to the delivery of welfare services we see a need for separatist women-controlled services for women's specific needs. Other services we believe must be transformed as part of a broader strategy to make welfare services more democratic and less professionalized and bureaucratized. Increasingly, the traditional Fabian and Marxist approaches to the reform of the Welfare State are being challenged from within the socialist movement as bureaucratic and centralist, and as concerned only with the quantity and distribution of public expenditure and services provided rather than the social relationships they embody. This new-left critique owes much to the women's movement.

In 1979 the authors of *Beyond the Fragments* (Rowbotham *et al.*, 1979) sent ripples through the socialist movement with their argument that the insights of feminism could form the basis for a new kind of organizing for socialism involving a movement of autonomous groups around a broad political programme embodying the demands and experiences of different groups.

In the mid-1980s the focus point of socialist campaigning has shifted to some local Labour Parties who are attempting to implement new policies of decentralized, participative services. The establishment of women's units is one form in which they have recognized feminism. It is equally important to remember that decentralized housing management or community development are feminist issues, since it has been the women in local communities who have always formed the backbone of local struggles against council policies which reduce the quality of life in their areas – for example the closure of local schools, the lack of repairs to local housing, dangerous roads and punitive rent rises.

In earlier chapters we attempted to understand the contradictory nature of the Welfare State for women. On the one hand, it does meet some of women's basic needs and has provided opportunities to improve women's overall position in society. On the other hand, feminists have demonstrated that many aspects of the Welfare State are oppressive for women. Their oppressions are experienced by *all* women in some form or other. We recognize, however, that for many black, working-class and lesbian women the specific effects of racial, class, and sexual oppression may give them different priorities in the struggle for liberation. Nevertheless, whilst respecting that different groups will define their own priorities, we believe that a broad based feminist strategy *can* encompass women's common interests. Abortion may be a greater priority for white, single women, but *all* women can agree on the demand for the right to control their own fertility.

We are a long way from achieving a non-sexist system of welfare provision which meets women's needs. The obstacles in our way – political, economic and cultural – are formidable, particularly in the current climate of attacks on women's rights. Nevertheless, feminists have some grounds for optimism. First, reforms have been achieved which we believe are, if not irreversible, unlikely to be reversed if current economic and social trends persist. Second, feminist activities have created sufficient change in attitudes to bring about a process of incremental change within state bureaucracies. At the time of going to press, a

Conclusion

High Court ruling has upheld an appeal by a married woman
that denial of Invalid Care Allowance contravenes the EEC ruling
against sex discrimination in social security benefits. Whether or
not the present government immediately concedes the principle,
there are likely to be more rulings in the future which will
eventually lead to some kind of response. Finally, although
radical change remains a very long-term goal, to a greater extent
than ever before, feminists insights will be an integral part of any
successful strategy to reverse the political dominance of the Right,
and move the Welfare State towards a true embodiment of the
principle of meeting human needs.

Bibliography

Abbot, E. and Bompas, K. (1943), *The Woman Citizen and Social Security*, Katherine Bompas, London.

Abel-Smith, B. (1960), *A History of the Nursing Profession*, Heinemann, London.

Ackland, J. W. (1982), *Girls in Care*, Gower, Aldershot.

Aitken-Swan, J. (1977), *Fertility, Control and the Medical Profession*, Croom Helm, London.

Albury, R. (1984), 'Who Owns the Embryo?', in Arditti *et al.* (eds.), *Test-Tube Women*, Pandora Press, London.

Amos, V. and Parmar, P. (1984), 'Challenging Imperial Feminism', in *Feminist Review*, no. 17, Autumn, pp. 3–19.

Arditti, R., Duelli Klein, R. and Minden, S. (1984), *Test-Tube Women*, Pandora Press, London.

Arnot, M. (1983), 'Educating Girls', in The Open University *The Changing Experience of Women*, Units 13 and 14, Open University Press, Milton Keynes.

Austerberry, H. and Watson, S. (1983), *Women on the Margins*, The Housing Research Group, City University, London.

Balbo, L. (1981), *The Patchwork Strategy: Coping and Resisting in the Crisis Society*, Mimeo.

Baly, M. (1973), *Nursing and Social Change*, Heinemann, London.

Banks, O. (1981), *Faces of Feminism*, Martin Robertson, Oxford.

Barrett, M. (1981), *Women's Oppression Today*, Verso, London.

Barrett, M. (1981b), 'Unity is Strength?', in *New Socialist*, no. 1, Sept.–Oct., pp. 35–8.

Barrett, M. and McIntosh, M. (1982), *The Anti-Social Family*, Verso, London.

Barrett, M. and Roberts, H. (1978), 'Doctors and their Patients: The Social Control of Women in General Practice', in Smart, C. and Smart, B. (eds), *Women's Sexuality and Social Control*, Routledge & Kegan Paul, London.

Belotti, E. (1975), *Little Girls*, Writers and Readers Publishing Cooperative, London.

Bennet, F. (1983), 'The State, Welfare and Women's Dependence', in Segal, L. (ed.), *What is to be Done About the Family?*, Penguin, Harmondsworth.

Bibliography

Berer, M. (1984), *Who Needs Depo Provera?*, Community Rights Projects, 157, Waterloo Road, London.

Bieggs, A. (1979), 'A Pig and A Poke', in *Scarlett Women* (10), Dec. 1979, pp. 8–9.

Binney, V., Harkell, G. and Nixon, J. (1981), *Leaving Violent Men*, Women's Aid Federation.

Bondfield, M. (1949), *A Life's Work*, Hutchinson, London.

Boyd, N. (1982), *Josephine Butler, Octavia Hill, Florence Nightingale*, Macmillan, London.

Briggs, A. (n.d.), *Who Cares*, Association of Carers.

Brion, M. and Tinker, A. (1980), *Women in Housing: Access and Influence*, Housing Centre Trust, London.

Brittain, V. (1953), *Lady into Woman*, Andrew Dakers, London.

Brophey, J. (1984), 'The "backlash" in family law: the Matrimonial and Family Proceedings Bill', in *Critical Social Policy*, vol. 4, no. 1, Summer, pp. 114–20.

Brownmiller, S. (1976), *Against Our Will: Men, Women and Rape*, Penguin, Harmondsworth.

Byrne, E. M. (1978), *Women and Education*, Tavistock Publications, London.

Campbell, B. (1980), 'United We Fall', in *Red Rag*, August.

Campbell, B. (1984), 'How the Other Half Lives', in *Marxism Today* vol. 28, no. 4, April, pp. 18–23.

Campbell, B. and Charlton, V. (1981), 'Work to Rule' in Feminist Anthology Collective. *No Turning Back*, The Women's Press, London.

Carpenter, M. (1977), 'The New Managerialism and Professionalism in Nursing', in Stacey, M., Reid, M., Heath, C. and Dingwall, R., *Health and the Division of Labour*, Croom Helm, London.

Carr, L. (1981), 'Access to the Curriculum', in *Equal Opportunities in Education*, NUT, London.

CHAC (1938), *The Management of Municipal Housing Estates*, HMSO, London.

Chesler, P. (1972), *Women and Madness*, Avon Books, New York.

Chew, D. N. (1982), *Ada Neild Chew, The Life and Writings of a Working Woman*, Virago, London.

Chodorow, N. (1978), *The Reproduction of Mothering*, University of California Press, Berkeley.

Cisler, L. (1970), 'Unfinished Business: Birth Control and Women's Liberation', in Morgan, R. (ed.), *Sisterhood is Powerful*, Vintage Books, New York.

Clarricoates, K. (1980), 'The Importance of Being Ernest . . . Emma . . . Tom . . . Jane. The Perception and Categorization of Gender Conformity and Gender Deviation in Primary Schools', in Deem, R. (ed.), *Women and Schooling*, Routledge & Kegan Paul, London.

Cockburn, C. (1977), *The Local State*, Pluto Press, London.

Coote, A. (1981), 'The A.E.S.: A New Starting Point', in *New Socialist*, no. 2, Nov.-Dec., pp. 4–7.

Coote, A. and Campbell, B. (1982), *Sweet Freedom. The Struggle for Women's Liberation*, Picador, London.

Corea, G. (1977), *The Hidden Malpractice,* Harcourt, Brace Jovanovich, New York.

Dalla Costa, M. and James, S. (1972), *The Power of Women and the Subversion of the Community*, Falling Wall Press, Bristol.

Dally, A. (1982), *Inventing Motherhood*, Burnett Books, London.

Daly, M. (1979), *Gyn/Ecology*, The Women's Press, London.

David, M. (1983), 'Sex Education and Social Policy: A New Moral Economy?', in Walker, S. and Barton, L. (eds), *Gender, Class and Education*, The Falmer Press, Sussex.

David, M. (1985), 'Motherhood and Social Policy – A Matter of Education?', in *Critical Social Policy*, vol. 4, no. 3, Spring, pp. 28-43.

Davies, L. (1983), 'Gender, Resistance and Power', in Walker, S. and Barton, L. (eds), *Gender, Class and Education*, The Falmer Press, Sussex.

Davies, M. L. (1978), *Maternity: Letters From Working Women*, Virago, London.

Deacon, A. (1976), *In Search of the Scrounger*, Bell, London.

Deem, R. (1978), *Women and Schooling*, Routledge & Kegan Paul, London.

Delamont, S. (1980), *Sex Roles and the School*, Methuen, London.

Delphy, C. (1984), *Close to Home*, Hutchinson, London.

DES (1963), *Half Our Future* (Newsom Report), HMSO, London.

DES (1975), *Curricular Differences Between the Sexes in Education*, Survey 21, HMSO, London.

DHSS (1978), *Social Assistance*, HMSO, London.

DHSS (1983), *Review of the Household Duties Test*, HMSO, London.

Dingwall, R. (1977), 'Collectivism, Regionalism and Feminism: Health Visiting and British Social Policy, 1850-1975', in *Journal of Social Policy*, vol. 6, no. 3, pp. 291-315.

Donnison, J. (1977), *Midwives and Medical Men*, Heinemann, London.

Donzelot, J. (1980), *The Policing of Families*, Hutchinson, London.

Doyal, L. (1979), *The Political Economy of Health*, Pluto Press, London.

Doyal, L. (1983), 'Women, Health and the Sexual Division of Labour: A Case Study of the Women's Health Movement in Britain', in *Critical Social Policy*, Issue 7, Summer, pp. 21-33.

Dreifus, C. (1977), 'Sterilising The Poor', in Dreifus, C. (ed.), *Seizing Our Bodies; The Politics of Women's Health*, Vintage Books, New York.

Ehrenreich, B. and English, D. (1973), *Complaints and Disorders: The Sexual Politics of Sickness*, Writers and Readers Publishing Cooperative, London.

Ehrenreich, B. and English, D. (1973b), *Witches, Midwives and Nurses: A History of Women's Health*, The Feminist Press, Old Westbury.

Ehrenreich, B. and English, D. (1979), *For Her Own Good: 150 Years of the Experts' Advice to Women*, Pluto Press, London.

Eisenstein, Z. (1981), *The Radical Future of Liberal Feminism*, Longman, New York.

Engels, F. (1972), *The Origins of the Family, Private Property and the State*, Pathfinder, New York.

EOC (1977), *Second Annual Report*, EOC, Manchester.

EOC (1979), *Do You Provide Equal Educational Opportunities?*, EOC, Manchester.

EOC (1980), *The Experience of Caring for Elderly and Handicapped Dependants: Survey Report*, EOC, Manchester.

EOC (1981a), *Education of Girls – A Statistical Analysis*, EOC, Manchester.

EOC (1981b), *Behind Closed Doors*, EOC, Manchester.

EOC (1982), *7th Annual Report*, EOC, Manchester.

EOC (1983a), *Equal Opportunities in the Classroom*, EOC, Manchester.

EOC (1983b), *Equality Now* (1), Autumn, EOC, Manchester.

EOC (1984), *What is W.I.S.E. Year All About?*, EOC, Manchester.

Fairbairns, Z. (1981), 'A Living Income', in Feminist Anthology Collective. *No Turning Back*, The Women's Press, London.

Family Policy Studies Centre (1984), *The Forgotten Army, Family Care and Elderly People*, FPSC, London.

Feminist Anthology Collective (1981), *No Turning Back*, The Women's Press, London.

Field, F. (1980), *Fair Shares For Families: The Need for a Family Impact Statement*, Study Commission on the Family, London.

Bibliography

Finch, J. (1984), 'Community Care: Developing Non-Sexist Alternatives', in *Critical Social Policy*, Issue 9, Spring, pp. 6–18.

Finch, J. (1985), 'A Response to Robert Harris', in *Critical Social Policy*, vol. 4, no. 3, Spring, pp. 123–6.

Finch, J. and Groves, D. (1980), 'Community Care and the Family', in *Journal of Social Policy*, vol. 9, Pt 4, October, pp. 487–511.

Finch, J. and Groves, D. (eds) (1983), *A Labour of Love: Women Work and Caring*, Routledge & Kegan Paul, London.

Firestone, S. (1979), *The Dialectic of Sex*, The Women's Press, London.

Fleming, S. (1975), 'Family Allowance: The Women's Money', in Edmond, W. and Fleming, S. (eds), *All Work and No Pay. Women, Housework and the Wages Due*, Power of Women Collective, Falling Wall Press, Bristol.

Friedan, B. (1965), *The Feminine Mystique*, Penguin, Harmondsworth.

Friedan, B. (1983), *The Second Stage*, Sphere Books, London.

Fry, V. and Morris, N. (1984), 'For Richer or Poorer', in *The Guardian*, London, 18.1.1984.

Gaffin, J. and Thoms, D. (1983), *Caring and Sharing: The Centenary History of the Cooperative Women's Guild*, Cooperative Union Ltd., Manchester.

Gardiner, J. and Smith, S. (1982), 'Feminism and the AES' in *Socialist Economic Review 1982*, pp. 31–45.

Gates, M. (1938), 'Women's Organisations During the Past Century', in *Manchester and Salford Woman Citizen*, July, pp. 10–11.

Gavron, H. (1966), *The Captive Wife*, Routledge & Kegan Paul, London.

George, V. (1968), *Social Security: Beveridge and After*, Routledge & Kegan Paul, London.

Glucklich, P. and Snell, M. (undated), *Women: Work and Wages*, Low Pay Unit Discussion Series No. 2, London.

Graham, H. (1983), 'Caring: A Labour of Love', in Finch, J. and Groves, D. (eds), *A Labour of Love: Women Work and Caring*, Routledge & Kegan Paul, London.

Graham, H. and Oakley, A. (1981), 'Competing Ideologies of Reproduction: Medical and Maternal Perspectives on Pregnancy', in Roberts, H. (ed.), *Women Health and Reproduction*, Routledge & Kegan Paul, London.

Grant, M. (1983), 'Craft, Design and Technology', in Whyld, J. (ed.), *Sexism in the Secondary Curriculum*, Harper & Row, London.

Gray, J. (1981), 'A Biological Basis for Sex Differences in Achievement in Science?', in Kelly, A. (ed.), *The Missing Half*, Manchester University Press, Manchester.

Hale, J. (1983), 'Feminism and Social Work Practice', in Jordan, W. and Parton, N., *The Political Dimension of Social Work*, pp. 167–87. Blackwell, Oxford.

Harris, R. (1985), 'End Points and Starting Points', in *Critical Social Policy*, vol. 4, No. 3., Spring, pp. 115–22.

Harrison, A. and Gretton, J. (1984), *Health Care UK 1984*, Chartered Institute of Public Finance and Accountancy, London.

Hartmann, H. (1981), 'The Unhappy Marriage of Marxism and Feminism', in *Capital and Class* no. 8.

Himmelweit, S. (1983), 'Production Rules OK? Waged Work and the Family', in Segal, L. (ed.), *What is to be Done About the Family?*, Penguin, Harmondsworth.

Howell, M. (1975), 'A Women's Health School?' *Social Policy*, vol. 6, no. 2, Sept.–Oct., pp. 50–3.

Howkins, J. and Bourne, G. (1971), *Shaw's Textbook of Gynaecology*, Ninth Edition, Churchill Livingstone, Edinburgh.

Hubbard, R. (1984), 'Personal Courage is Not Enough: Some Hazards of

Childbearing in the 1980's' in Arditti *et al.* (eds), *Test Tube Women*, Pandora Press, London.

Hudson, A. (1983), 'The Welfare State and Adolescent Feminity', in *Youth and Policy*, vol. 2, no. 1, Summer, pp. 5–13.

Hudson, A. (1984), 'Feminism and Social Work: Resistance or Dialogue?', unpublished draft, Dept. Social Administration, University of Manchester.

Hunt, A. (1978), *The Elderly at Home*, HMSO, London.

James, S. (1976), *Women, the Unions and Work, or . . . What is not to be done and the Perspective of Winning*, London Wages for Housework Committee, Falling Wall Press, Bristol.

Jeffcoate, N. (1975), *Principles of Gynaecology*, Fourth Edition, Butterworth, London.

Jex-Blake, S. (1886), *Medical Women: A Thesis and a History*, Oliphant Anderson and Ferrier, Edinburgh.

Jones, H. (ed.) (1975), *Towards a New Social Work*, Routledge & Kegan Paul, London.

Jordan, W. (1981), 'Family Therapy – An Outsider's View', in *Journal of Family Therapy*, vol. 3, no. 3, Aug., pp. 269–80.

Kelly, A. (ed.) (1981), *The Missing Half*, Manchester University Press, Manchester.

Kelly, A. (1982), 'Why Girls Don't Do Science', in *New Scientist*, 20 May, pp. 497–500, extract in Arnot, M., *The Changing Experience of Women*, Open University Press, Milton Keynes.

Klein, R. (1984), 'Doing it Ourselves: Self-Insemination', in Arditti *et al.* (eds), *Test-Tube Women*, Pandora Press, London.

Land, H. (1978), 'Who Cares for the Family?', in *Journal of Social Policy*, vol. 7, no. 3, July, pp. 257–84.

Larsen, B. (1983), 'Geography', in Whyld, J., (ed.), *Sexism in the Secondary Curriculum*, Harper & Row, London.

Leeds Revolutionary Feminist Group (1982), 'Political Lesbianism: The Case Against Heterosexuality', in Evans, M. (ed) *The Woman Question*, Fontana, London.

Leeson, J. and Gray, J. (1978), *Women and Medicine*, Tavistock, London.

Lewis, J. (1980), *The Politics of Motherhood*, Croom Helm, London.

Lister, R. (1973), *As Man and Wife?*, Poverty Research Series 2, CPAG, London.

Lobban, G. (1976), 'Sex Roles in Reading Schemes', in Children's Rights Workshop, *Sexism in Children's Books*, Writers and Readers Publishing Cooperative, London.

Local Government Operational Research Unit (1984), *Developing the Neglected Resource: An Action Report*, LGORU, Reading.

London Edinburgh Weekend Return Group (1979), *In and Against the State*, Pluto Press, London.

London Women's Liberation Campaign for Legal and Financial Independence and Rights of Women (1979), 'Disaggregation Now! Another Battle for Women's Independence', in *Feminist Review*, no. 2, pp. 19–31.

MacIntyre, S. (1976), 'Who Wants Babies? The Social Construction of Instincts', in Barker, D. and Allen, S. (eds), *Sexual Divisions and Society: Process and Change*, Tavistock, London.

MacIntyre, S. and Oldman, D. (1977), 'Coping With Migraine', in Davis, A. and Horobin, G., *Medical Encounters*, Croom Helm, London.

Macnicol, J. (1980), *The Movement for Family Allowances, 1918–1945*, Heinemann, London.

Malos, E. (ed) (1980), *The Politics of Housework*, Alison and Busby, London.

Manchester's Community Health Councils (1981), *Well-Women Clinics – Proposals for Manchester*, Manchester's Community Health Councils, Manchester.

Bibliography

Manchester's Community Health Councils (1983), *National Guidelines for Well-Women Centres*, Manchester Community Health Councils, Manchester.

Martin, A. (1911), *The Married Working Woman*, NUWSS, London.

Massey, D. and Morgan, R. (1982), *The Anatomy of Job Loss*, Methuen, London.

Ministry of Reconstruction (1918), *First Interim Report of the Women's Housing Sub-Committee*, Cd. 9166, HMSO, London.

Ministry of Reconstruction (1919), *Final Report of the Women's Housing Sub-Committee*, Cmnd 9232, HMSO, London.

Mitchell, J. (1974), *Psychoanalysis and Feminism*, Allen Lane, London.

Murie, A. (1983), *Housing Inequality and Deprivation*, Heinemann, London.

Nairne, K. and Smith, B. (1984), *Dealing With Depression*, Women's Press, London.

Nava, M. (1983), 'From Utopian to Scientific Feminism? Early Feminist Critiques of the Family', in Segal, L. (ed), *What is to be Done About the Family?*, Penguin, Harmondsworth.

Newsom, J. (1948), *The Education of Girls*, Faber & Faber, London.

Novak, E., Jones, G. and Jones, J. (1975), *Gynecology*, Williams and Wilkins Co., Baltimore.

NUSEC (1927), *Statement of Views on Immediate Programme by Those Standing for Election to the Executive Committee*, NUSEC, London.

NWAF (1980), *Annual Report 1979–80*, NWAF, London.

NWAF (1978), *Half the Sky – and Still No Roof*, NWAF and Welsh Women's Aid, London and Cardiff.

Oakley, A. (1974), *Housewife*, Penguin, Harmondsworth.

Oliver, J. (1982), in *Community Care*, December, pp. 15–16.

Oliver, J. (1983), 'The Caring Wife', in Finch, J. and Groves, D. (eds), *A Labour of Love: Women Work and Caring*, Routledge & Kegan Paul, London.

Onians, S. (1983), 'Britain's Missing Half', in *Technology*, 14 March 83, pp. 14–16.

O'Sullivan, S. (1975), 'Sterilisation', in *Spare Rib*, no. 33, March, pp. 10–13.

Over 21 (March, 1984), Special Survey Report, 'Doctors and You', pp. 22–3.

Overfield, K. (1981), 'Dirty Fingers, Grime and Slag Heaps: Purity and the Scientific Ethic', in Spender, D. (ed.). *Men's Studies Modified*, Pergamon Press, Oxford.

Page, E., Villee, C. and Villee, D. (1976), *Human Reproduction*, 2nd Edition, W. B. Saunders, Philadelphia.

Pahl, J. (1978), *A Refuge for Battered Women*, HMSO London.

Pahl, J. (1980), 'Patterns of Money Management in Marriage' in *Journal of Social Policy*, vol. 9, no. 3, pp. 313–35.

Piachaud, D. (1982), *Family Incomes Since the War*, Study Commission on the Family, London.

Piercy, M. (1980), *Woman on the Edge of Time*, The Women's Press, London.

Pizzey, E. and Shapiro, J. (1982), *Prone To Violence*, Hamlyn, Feltham.

Popay, J., Rimmer, L. and Rossiter, C. (1983), *One Parent Families*, Study Commission on the Family, London.

Popplestone, R. (1980), 'Top Jobs For Women: Are the Cards Stacked Against Them?', *Social Work Today*, vol. 12, no. 4, 23.9.80, pp. 12–15.

Prochaska, F. K. (1980), *Women and Philanthropy in Nineteenth Century England*, Clarendon, Oxford.

Rakusen, J. (1982), 'Feminism and the Politics of Health', in *Medicine in Society*, vol. 8, no. 1, pp. 17–25.

Rathbone, E. (1929), *Milestones. Presidential Addresses at the Annual Council Meetings of the NUSEC by Eleanor Rathbone. 1920–1929*, NUSEC, London.

Ravetz, M. (1974), *Model Estate: Planned Housing at Quarry Hill, Leeds*, Croom Helm, London.

Reiss, L. (1935), 'A Woman in Charge', in *Manchester and Salford Woman Citizen*, February.
Richards, B. (1979), 'The Myths of Sexual Medicine', in *World Medicine*, 10.3.79, pp. 51-3.
Richards, J. R. (1982), *The Sceptical Feminist*, Penguin, Harmondsworth.
Richards, J. R. (1983), 'Why Should Women have the Monopoly on Virtue', in *The Guardian*, 10.5.83.
Riley, D. (1983a), *War in the Nursery*, Virago, London.
Riley, D. (1983b), 'The Serious Burden of Love? Some Questions on Child-Care Feminism and Socialism', in Segal, L. (ed.), *What is to be Done About the Family?*, Penguin, Harmondsworth.
Roberts, H. (ed) (1981), *Women Health and Reproduction*, Routledge & Kegan Paul, London.
Roggencamp, V. (1984), 'Abortion of a Special Kind: Male Sex Selection in India', in Arditti *et al.* (eds.), *Test-Tube Women*, Pandora Press, London.
Roth, R. and Lerner, J. (1974), 'Sex Based Discrimination in the Mental Institutionalisation of Women', in *California Law Review 62*, pp. 789-815.
Rothman, B. (1984), 'The Meanings of Choice in Reproductive Technology', in Arditti *et al.* (eds) *Test-Tube Women*, Pandora Press, London.
R.O.W. (1979) *Women and Income Tax*, ROW, London.
R.O.W. (1984), *Lesbian Mothers on Trial*, ROW, London.
Rowbotham, S. (1973a), *Hidden From History*, Pluto Press, London.
Rowbotham, S. (1973b), *Women's Consciousness, Man's World*, Penguin, Harmondsworth.
Rowbotham, S. (1981), 'The Trouble with "Patriarchy"', in Feminist Anthology Collective. *No Turning Back*, The Women's Press, London.
Rowbotham, S., Segal, L. and Wainwright, H. (1979), *Beyond the Fragments*, Merlin Press, London.
Royal Commission for Inquiring into the Housing of the Working Classes (1885), *First Report*, C.4402, HMSO, London.
Ruzek, S. B. (1978), *The Women's Health Movement*, Praeger, New York.
Seaman, B. (1975a), 'Pelvic Autonomy: Four Proposals', in *Social Policy*, Sept-Oct., pp. 43-7.
Seaman, B. (1975b), quoted by Corea, G. (1977), *The Hidden Malpractice*, Jove, New York.
Segal, L. (ed.) (1983), *What is to be Done About the Family?* Penguin, Harmondsworth.
Sharpe, S. (1976), *Just Like A Girl*, Penguin, Harmondsworth.
Sheffield Black Women's Group (1984), 'Black Women - What Kind of Health Care Can We Expect in Racist Britain?', in Kanter, H. *et al.* (ed), *Sweeping Statements*, The Women's Press, London.
Smith, D. (1978), 'A Peculiar Eclipsing: Women's Exclusion from Man's Culture', in *Women's Studies International Quarterly*, vol. 1, no. 4, pp. 281-96.
Smith, E. (1981), 'The Problem of "Equal Pay for Equal Work" in Great Britain during World War Two', in *Journal of Modern History*, vol 53, no. 4, December, pp. 652-72.
Social Insurance and Allied Services: Report by Sir William Beveridge (1942), Cmd. 6404, HMSO, p. 19.
Social Insurance and Allied Services: Memoranda from Organisations (1942), Cmd. 6405, HMSO, London.
Spare Rib (1978), 'Schoolgirls up Against Sexism', Issue 75, October, pp. 6-8.
Spender, D. (1980), in Spender, D. and Sarah, E. (1980), *Learning to Lose: Sexism and Education*, The Women's Press, London.

Bibliography

Spender, D. (1981), 'Sex Bias' in Warren Piper, D. (ed.), *Is Higher Education Fair?*, Society for Research into Higher Education, Guildford, Surrey.

Spender, D. (1982), *Invisible Women: The Schooling Scandal*, Writers and Readers Publishing Cooperative, London.

Spender, D. (1983a), *Women of Ideas*, Routledge & Kegan Paul, London.

Spender, D. (1983b), *There's Always Been a Women's Movement This Century*, Pandora Press, London.

Stacey, M. and Price, M. (1981), *Women, Power and Politics*, Tavistock, London.

Stanworth, M. (1983), *Gender and Schooling*, Hutchinson, London.

Strachey, R. (1978), *The Cause*, Virago, London.

Taylor, B. (1983), *Eve and the New Jerusalem*, Virago, London.

Thatcher, M. (1973), Select Committee on Anti-Discrimination (no. 2) Bill, *Special Report*, H.C. 331-1, pp. 38–49, HMSO, London.

Traynor, J. and Hasnip, J. (1984), 'Sometimes She Makes Me Want to Hit Her', in *Community Care*, 2.8.84, pp. 20–1.

Tunnadine, D. and Green, R. (1978), *Unwanted Pregnancy – Accident or Illness*, Oxford University Press, Oxford.

Turnbull, A., Pollock, J. and Bruley, S. (1983), 'History', in Whyld, J. (ed), *Sexism in the Secondary Curriculum*, Harper & Row, London.

Veevers, J. (1980), *Childless By Choice*, Butterworth and Co., Toronto and London.

Walford, G. (1980), 'Sex Bias in Physics Textbooks', School Science Review, vol. 62, December, quoted in Whyld, J. (ed), *Sexism in the Secondary Curriculum*, Harper & Row, London.

Walker, A. (1983), 'Care for Elderly People: A Conflict Between Women and the State', in Finch, J. and Groves, D. (eds), *A Labour of Love: Women Work and Caring*, Routledge & Kegan Paul, London.

Walker, J., MacGillivary, I. and MacNaughton, M. (1976), *Combined Textbook of Obstetrics and Gynaecology*, Ninth Edition, Churchill Livingstone, Edinburgh.

Walker, P. (1984), quoted in *The Guardian*, 11.4.84, p. 3.

Walker, S. and Barton, L. (eds) (1983), *Gender, Class and Education*, The Falmer Press, Sussex.

Walsh, M. R. (1977), *Doctors Wanted: No Women Need Apply*, Yale University Press, London.

Walton, R. (1975), *Women in Social Work*, Routledge & Kegan Paul, London.

Watson, S. (1983), 'On the State-Non State Divide, Another Perspective', in *Critical Social Policy*, vol. 2, no. 3, pp. 96–9.

Watson, S. and Austerberry, H. (1980), 'A Woman's Place: A Feminist Approach to Housing in Britain', in *Feminist Review*.

Weir, A. and McIntosh, M. (1982), 'Towards a Wages Strategy For Women', in *Feminist Review*, Spring.

Wheatcroft, M. (ed.) (1960), *Housework with Satisfaction*, National Council for Social Service, London.

Whyld, J. (ed) (1983), *Sexism in the Secondary Curriculum*, Harper & Row, London.

Willcocks, D., Peace, S. and Kellaher, L. (1982), *The Residential Life of Old People: A Study in 100 Local Authority Homes*, Survey Research Unit, Polytechnic of North London, London.

Wilson, E. (1977), *Women and the Welfare State*, Tavistock, London.

Wilson, E. (1980), *Only Halfway to Paradise*, Tavistock, London.

Wilson, E. (1982), 'Women, the "Community" and the "Family"', in Walker, A. (ed.), (1982), *Community Care: the Family, the State and Social Policy*, Blackwell and Robertson, Oxford.

Wilson, E. (1983), *What is to be Done About Violence Against Women?* Penguin, Harmondsworth.

Women's Freedom League (1908), *Verbatim Report of a Debate on December 3rd. 1907. Sex Equality (Teresa Billington-Grieg) versus Adult Suffrage (Margaret Bondfield)*, WFL, London.

Woodroofe, K. (1962), *From Charity to Social Work in England and the United States*, Routledge & Kegan Paul, London.

Wormald, E. (1982), 'Political Participation' in Reid, I. and Wormald, E., *Sex Differences in Britain*, Grant McIntyre, London.

Wynn, B. (1983), 'Home Economics', in Whyld, J. (ed.), *Sexism in the Secondary Curriculum*, Harper & Row, London.

Young, G. (1981), 'A Woman in Medicine: Reflections From the Inside', in Roberts, H. (ed.), *Women Health and Reproduction*, Routledge & Kegan Paul, London.

Index

Index

Equal Pay Act 1970, 43, 119, 131-2, 173
Equal Pay Campaign Committee, 17, 19
European Economic Community, 106, 108-9, 119-20, 132

Fabians, x, 114, 178
Fairbairn, Z., 128, 129
the family: ideology of, 60-1, 108, 111; and women's oppression, 47-8, 99; *see also* carers, child care, motherhood
Family Allowance Campaign, 130
Family Allowances, 10, 12, 16, 119, 130; *see also* child benefit
Family Endowment Society, 12
Family Policy Studies Centre, 111
Family Therapy, 97
family wage, 12, 119
Feminists, *see* Feminist Welfare Professionals; Liberal Feminists; Radical Feminists; Social Feminists
feminist theory, 51-60; biology in, 51-3; class in, 51, 54, 65-7; psychoanalysis and, 63-4; *see also* patriarchy
feminist welfare professionals: in education, 142, 145, 176; in medicine, 141, 146; in social work, 101, 141, 147
Finch, J., 113
Finch, J. and Groves, D., 112
Firestone, S., 51, 89
Fleming, S., 130
Friedan, B., 44, 45, 117

Gaffin, J. and Thomas, D., 13
Garrett, E., 25
Garrett Fawcett, M., 6
Gavron, H., 46
George, H., 46
George, V., 106
Gillick, V., 102
girls and science, 69, 75-6, 78, 143
Glucklich, P. and Snell, M., 131
GPs, 84-5, 92, 94, 147
Graham, H., 64

Graham, H., and Oakley, A., 94, 95
Grant, M., 143, 144
Gray, J., 165
gynaecologists/obstetricians, 83-8, 90-1, 94, 146-8

Hale, J., 95-6, 99, 141
Harris, R., 113
Harrison, A. and Gretton, J., 146
Hartmann, H., 56, 58
health visitors, 13, 21, 29, 35-7
Hill, Octavia, 29-31, 34
Himmelweit, S., 125
Hirsch, J., 158
homelessness, 115, 116
housewives, 17, 46, 92
Housewives Non-Contributory Invalidity Pension, 109
housework, 44-5, 93, 106, 109, 117, 125; *see also* domestic labour debate: wages for housework
housing: access to housing, 114-16; house design, 14, 116-17; housing management, 21, 29-33
Howell, M., 160
Hubbard, R., 91
Hudson, A., 98-9, 141
Hunt, A., 112
Huntingford, P., 147

ILEA, 72, 143-4
incest, 98, 99
incomes policy, 119, 132
induction, 94
infertility treatment, 90-4
Institute of Housing, 32, 33
Invalid Care Allowance, 109, 129-30

James, S., 125-7
Jeffcoate, N., 84, 86
Jex-Blake, S., 23-5
Jones, H., 97
Jordan, W., 97

Kelly, A., 63, 72, 75-6
Kitzinger, S., 94
Klein, R., 89

192

Index